CCCC
KICK THE HABIT

A UN GUIDE TO
CLIMATE NEUTRALITY

WRITER Alex Kirby

UNEP/GRID-ARENDAL EDITORIAL TEAM Jasmina Bogdanovic
Claudia Heberlein
Otto Simonett
Christina Stuhlberger

CARTO-GRAPHICS Emmanuelle Bournay

COPY EDITING Harry Forster, Interrelate Grenoble

A CLIMATE NEUTRAL BOOK...

The production and transport of each copy of this book has released about 5 kilos of CO_2 equivalent into the atmosphere. This value is comparable to the amount of CO_2 generated when burning 2 litres of petrol. Factors that have been taken into consideration for this calculation are shipping (40 per cent), staff and editorial board travel (20 per cent), paper (20 per cent), printing (13 per cent) and energy consumption for office and computer use (7 per cent).

The use of sustainably produced recycled paper and plant-based ink helped to lower the climate impact, whearas the transport of 500 copies to New Zealand for book launch is responsible for the biggest chunk of emissions.

myclimate

In order to compensate the total amount of 26 tonnes CO_2 equivalent generated by the project, we purchased the according amount of carbon offsets with the help of the Swiss non-profit foundation myclimate. The money will be invested in the Te Apiti wind energy farm in New Zealand, a Gold Standard Joint Implementation project.

KICK THE HABIT

Foreword

Addiction is a terrible thing. It consumes and controls us, makes us deny important truths and blinds us to the consequences of our actions. Our society is in the grip of a dangerous greenhouse gas habit.

Coal and oil paved the way for the developed world's industrial progress. Fast-developing countries are now taking the same path in search of equal living standards. Meanwhile, in the least developed countries, even less sustainable energy sources, such as charcoal, remain the only available option for the poor.

Our dependence on carbon-based energy has caused a significant build-up of greenhouse gases in the atmosphere. Last year, the Nobel Peace Prize-winning Intergovernmental Panel on Climate Change (IPCC) put the final nail in the coffin of global warming skeptics. We know that climate change is happening, and we know that carbon dioxide (CO_2) and other greenhouse gases that we emit are the cause.

We don't just burn carbon in the form of fossil fuels. Throughout the tropics, valuable forests are being felled for timber and making paper, for pasture and arable land and, increasingly, for plantations to supply a growing demand for biofuels. This further manifestation of our greenhouse gas habit is not only releasing vast amounts of CO_2, it is destroying a valuable resource for absorbing atmospheric CO_2, further contributing to climate change.

The environmental, economic and political implications of global warming are profound. Ecosystems – from mountain to ocean, from the Poles to the tropics – are undergoing rapid change. Low-lying cities face inundation, fertile lands are turning to desert, and weather patterns are becoming ever more unpredictable.

The cost will be borne by all. The poor will be hardest hit by weather-related disasters and by soaring price inflation for staple foods, but even the richest nations face the prospect of economic recession and a world in conflict over diminishing resources. Mitigating climate change, eradicating poverty and promoting economic and political stability all demand the same solution: we must kick the carbon habit.

Kicking the habit is the theme of this book. Written in easy to understand language, but based on the most up-to-date science and policy, it is a guide for governments, organizations small and large, businesses and individuals who want to embark on the path to climate neutrality.

From reducing consumption and increasing energy efficiency, to offsetting emissions via the multitude of carbon trading schemes – including the Kyoto Protocol's Clean Development Mechanism – the opportunities are plentiful.

The fundamental message of "Kick the Habit – A UN Guide to Climate Neutrality" is that we are all part of the solution. Whether you are an individual, a business, an organization or a government, there are many steps you can take to reduce your climate footprint. It is a message we all must take to heart.

Ban Ki-moon
Secretary-General of the United Nations

Climate change
global processes and effects

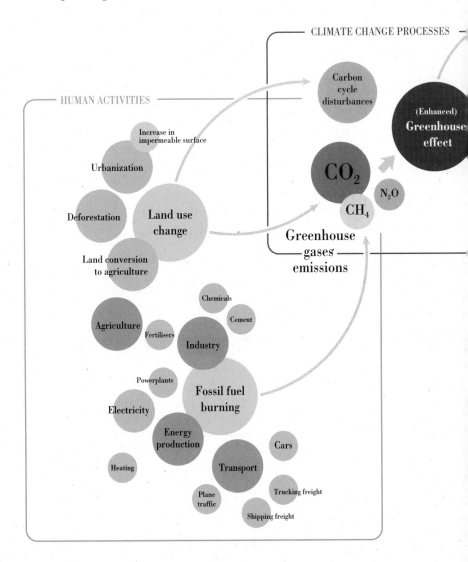

HUMAN ACTIVITIES

Increase in impermeable surface

Urbanization

Deforestation

Land use change

Land conversion to agriculture

Carbon cycle disturbances

(Enhanced) Greenhouse effect

CO_2

N_2O

CH_4

Greenhouse gases emissions

Chemicals

Cement

Agriculture

Fertilisers

Industry

Powerplants

Electricity

Fossil fuel burning

Energy production

Cars

Heating

Transport

Plane traffic

Trucking freight

Shipping freight

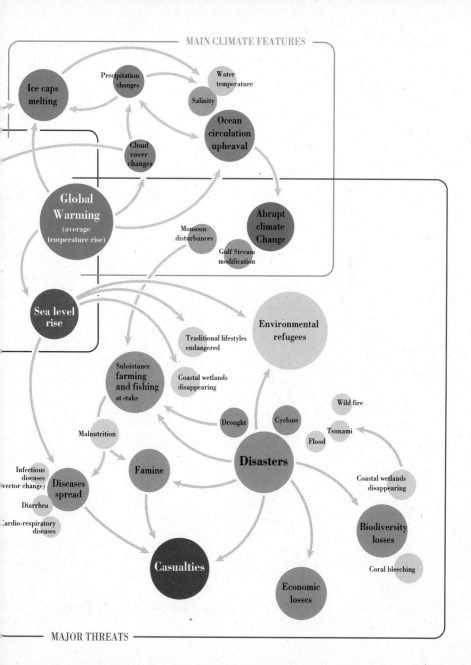

Ice caps melting

Precipitation changes

Water temperature

Salinity

Ocean circulation upheaval

Cloud cover changes

Global Warming (average temperature rise)

Monsoon disturbances

Abrupt climate Change

Gulf Stream modification

Sea level rise

Traditional lifestyles endangered

Environmental refugees

Subsistance farming and fishing at stake

Coastal wetlands disappearing

Malnutrition

Drought

Cyclone

Wild fire

Tsunami

Flood

Infectious diseases (vector change)

Diseases spread

Famine

Disasters

Coastal wetlands disappearing

Diarrhea

Cardio-respiratory diseases

Biodiversity losses

Casualties

Coral bleaching

Economic losses

Yearly emissions of the average World Citizen

4 080

Examples of GHG emission amounts generated by different activities or goods are scattered across the book in the form of proportional bubbles (in kilograms of CO_2 equivalent).

Sources: ADEME, Bilan Carbone® Entreprises et Collectivités, Guide des facteurs d'émissions, 2007; US Environmental Protection Agency (www.epa.gov/solar/energy-resources/calculator.html); ESU-Services Consulting (Switzerland); World Wildlife Fund; Jean-Marc Manicore (www.manicore.com); Jean-Pierre Bourdier (www.x-environnement.org); fatknowledge.blogspot.com; www.actu-environnement.com; www.cleanair-coolplanet.org.

23 Running a TV for a year

9 Running a compter for hours

565 Treating one cubic metre of **wastewater** from **sugar production**

59 Treating one cubic metre of **wastewater** from a **brewery**

CCCC

KICK THE HABIT

INTRODUCTION

Climate change is the defining issue of our era. Hardly a day passes without a newspaper, a broadcast or a politician making at least one reference to the threats it poses and the urgency of taking action, immediately to limit the effects and, in the longer term, to adapt to the changes that are sure to come.

For climate change is upon us, and the problem is here to stay. But it is still in our power – as individuals, businesses, cities and governments – to influence just how serious the problem will become. We have the choice how to act, but the change we need to make ourselves. We can make a difference by supporting the transition to a climate-neutral world. This concept – climate neutrality – is the subject of this book.

True, there is a huge gulf between where we are now and the climate-neutral future that we need if we are to achieve sustainable development. But the message of this book is that the gulf is not uncrossable and that there is also a lot to gain. It will take patience, persistence and determination, but it can be done.

There is plenty of information and advice about how to live a greener, cleaner life. What is often difficult is finding your way through it all – knowing what gets results fast, what really delivers instead of just being greenwash, and what works best for you. If you are confused, this book is certainly for you. It should provide the answers you want. It explains in practical terms how individuals, companies, corporations, cities and countries can start to change. And even if you are not confused, the book will provide you with some useful additional information.

Climate neutrality

The term **climate neutrality** is used in this book to mean living in a way

> Carbon-neutral, yes – that sounds familiar. But climate? The answer is simple: it is not just carbon dioxide, CO_2, that is driving climate change, even if it makes up almost 80 per cent of the climate gases (including contributions from changes in land use) emitted by human activities. Carbon dioxide is the most abundant greenhouse gas we are adding to the atmosphere, but it is not the only one.
>
> The international climate change treaty, the Kyoto Protocol, limits the emissions of six main GHGs produced by human activities (see table). The gases are carbon dioxide (CO_2), methane (CH_4), nitrous oxide (N_2O), hydrofluorocarbons (HFC), perfluorocarbons (PFC), and sulphur hexafluoride (SF_6).

which produces no net greenhouse gas (GHG) emissions. This should be achieved by reducing your own GHG emissions as much as possible, and using carbon offsets to neutralize the remaining emissions.

Kick the Habit – the analogy with a diet is apt: the commitment to try to lose weight comes quite close to what is needed to become climate-neutral. We need to kick the habit of releasing large quantities of GHGs. Of course, nobody diets for fun, but only in the hope of achieving something really worthwhile – perhaps a new slim and sexy you, perhaps the chance of survival itself. And diets are a reminder of something else involved in reducing GHGs. It is not an event but a process. No one embarks on a diet, loses weight, then resumes their old lifestyle – or at least, if they do then they can expect the whole exercise to prove pointless. So reducing the unnecessary consumption that underlies so much of many people's GHG emissions is not a question of aiming to cut your wasteful behaviour to a given point and then relaxing. The journey to climate neutrality is not a

Gas name	Pre-industrial concentration (ppmv *)	Concentration in 1998 (ppmv)	Atmospheric lifetime (years)	Main human activity source	GWP **
Water vapour	1 to 3	1 to 3	a few days	-	-
Carbon dioxide (CO_2)	280	365	variable	Fossil fuels, cement production, land use change	1
Methane (CH_4)	0,7	1,75	12	Fossil fuels, rice paddies waste dumps, livestock	21
Nitrous oxide (N_2O)	0,27	0,31	114	Fertilizers, combustion industrial processes	310
HFC 23 (CHF_3)	0	0,000014	250	Electronics, refrigerants	12 000
HFC 134 a (CF_3CH_2F)	0	0,0000075	13,8	Refrigerants	1 300
HFC 152 a (CH_3CHF_2)	0	0,0000005	1,4	Industrial processes	120
Perfluoromethane (CF_4)	0,0004	0,00008	>50 000	Aluminium production	5 700
Perfluoroethane (C_2F_6)	0	0,000003	10 000	Aluminium production	11 900
Sulphur hexafluoride (SF_6)	0	0,0000042	3 200	Dielectric fluid	22 200

* ppmv = parts per million by volume, ** GWP = Global warming potential (for 100 year time horizon).

straight line, but a cycle, a matter of slimming down the GHGs that are within our responsibility and offsetting the remainder. In the next round you look at how you can cut your own emissions further, and continue the cycle moving away from offsetting and towards reducing your own emissions in your balance. Going on a climate diet will not be exactly fun, either, though it may help us to rediscover the forgotten delights that come from doing more with less. But it will give us and future generations the hope of survival on a sustaining Earth.

Four reasons to become climate neutral

There are several good reasons for reducing our climate footprint.

One – sparing the climate

The build-up of GHGs threatens to set the Earth inexorably on the path to a unpredictably different climate. The Intergovernmental Panel on Climate Change **(IPCC)** says many parts of the planet will be warmer. Droughts,

> The United Nations Environment Programme and the World Meteorological Organization set up the IPCC, which brings together more than 2 000 scientists and government representatives to assess the risk posed by human-induced changes in climate. The IPCC does not itself conduct any research, nor does it monitor climate data. Its job is to assess the latest scientific, technical and socio-economic literature on understanding the risk of climate change, its observed and projected impacts, and options for adaptation and mitigation. In November 2007 it released its Fourth Assessment Report, comprising four sections: The Physical Science Basis, by Working Group I; Impacts, Adaptation and Vulnerability, by Working Group II; Mitigation of Climate Change, by Working Group III; and an overall Synthesis Report. It took six years to complete the report, which runs to several thousand pages. For this and its work over the last 20 years the IPCC was the joint winner of the 2007 Nobel Peace Prize.

floods and other forms of extreme weather will become more frequent, threatening food supplies. Plants and animals which cannot adjust will die out. Sea-levels are rising and will continue to do so, forcing hundreds of thousands of people in coastal zones to migrate. One of the main GHGs which humans are adding to the atmosphere, carbon dioxide (CO_2), is increasing rapidly. Around 1750, about the start of the Industrial Revolution in Europe, there were 280 parts per million (ppm) of CO_2 in the atmosphere. Today the overall amount of GHGs has topped 390 ppm CO_2e (parts per million of carbon dioxide equivalent – all GHGs expressed as a common metric in relation to their warming

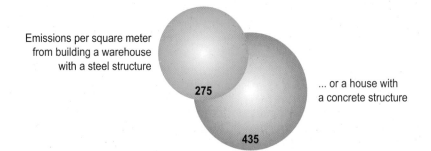

Emissions per square meter
from building a warehouse
with a steel structure

275

... or a house with
a concrete structure

435

Emissions by gas

Thousand million tonnes of CO_2 equivalent per year
(1970-2004 period)

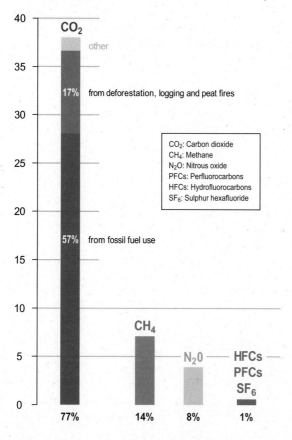

CO₂: Carbon dioxide
CH₄: Methane
N₂O: Nitrous oxide
PFCs: Perfluorocarbons
HFCs: Hydrofluorocarbons
SF₆: Sulphur hexafluoride

Source: IPCC Fourth Assessment Report, Working Group III Report: Mitigation of Climate Change; 2007
(figure adapted from Olivier et al., 2005; 2006; Hooijer et al., 2006).

Strategic options for climate change mitigation
Global cost curve for greenhouse gas abatement measures

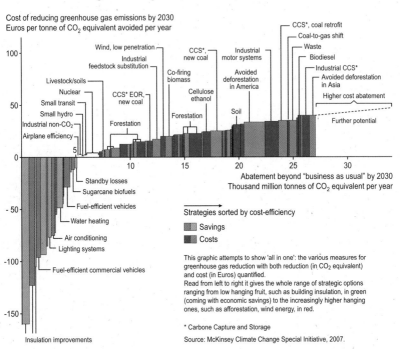

Cost of reducing greenhouse gas emissions by 2030
Euros per tonne of CO_2 equivalent avoided per year

Abatement beyond "business as usual" by 2030
Thousand million tonnes of CO_2 equivalent per year

Strategies sorted by cost-efficiency

Savings
Costs

This graphic attempts to show 'all in one': the various measures for greenhouse gas reduction with both reduction (in CO_2 equivalent) and cost (in Euros) quantified.
Read from left to right it gives the whole range of strategic options ranging from low hanging fruit, such as building insulation, in green (coming with economic savings) to the increasingly higher hanging ones, such as afforestation, wind energy, in red.

* Carbone Capture and Storage

Source: McKinsey Climate Change Special Initiative, 2007.

potential) and the figure is rising by 1.5–2 ppm annually. Reputable scientists believe the Earth's average temperature should not rise by more than 2°C over pre-industrial levels. Among others, the European Union indicated that this is essential to minimize the risk of what the UN Framework Convention for Climate Change calls dangerous climate change and keep the costs of adapting to a warmer world bearable. Scientists say there is a 50 per cent chance of keeping to 2°C if the total GHG concentration remains below 450 ppm.

Two – conserving natural resources

There is growing evidence of another and quite different threat developing: we may soon run short of the fossil fuels (gas and oil) which keep modern society going. Not only do they provide heat, light and electricity. Agriculture, pharmaceuticals, communications and most of the other features of life we take for granted depend on the reserves of fossil fuels, directly (e.g. for plastics) or indirectly. ASPO, the Association for the Study of Peak Oil and Gas, says: "The world faces the dawn of the second half of the age of oil, when this critical commodity, which plays such a fundamental part in the modern economy, heads into decline due to natural depletion." Some economists believe that the scarcer and more expensive a commodity becomes, the more effort will go into finding it, and that the market will ensure plentiful supplies of fossil fuel for many years ahead. But there are rational grounds for thinking we risk the exhaustion of recoverable reserves of oil and gas as well as an unpredictably warmer Earth if we do not kick the CO_2 habit. By 2030, projections suggest, world energy use will probably have increased by more than 50 per cent. We can attain energy security only if we move from fossil fuels to fossil free alternatives.

A related argument is that a growing human population is putting the Earth under increasing strain, and that it is in everyone's interest to try to reduce the strain. There were more than 6.6 thousand million people in the world in early 2008, and the UN Population Fund expects the total to reach about 9 thousand million before it starts to decline. Add to that a growing global appetite for consumer goods, and it becomes clear that unless we disconnect consumption and growing standards of living from the use of natural resources, we shall soon run short of many essential resources – minerals, like uranium, copper and gold, for example.

Extraction and refinery of crude oil
to make one tonne of petrol

570

Carbon cycle

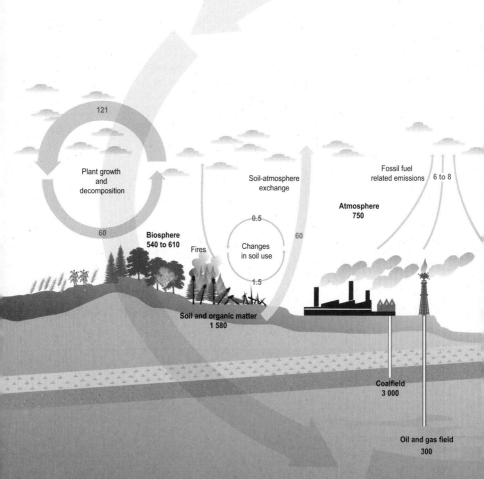

121

Plant growth
and
decomposition

60

Soil-atmosphere
exchange

Fossil fuel
related emissions   6 to 8

Atmosphere
750

0.5

**Biosphere
540 to 610**

Fires

Changes
in soil use

60

1.5

**Soil and organic matter
1 580**

**Coalfield
3 000**

**Oil and gas field
300**

Sources: Centre for Climatic Research, Institute for Environmental Studies,
University of Wisconsin at Madison (USA); Okanagan University College
(Canada), Geography Department; World Watch, November-December 1998;
Nature; Intergovernmental Panel on Climate Change, 2001 and 2007.

The figures indicate carbon storage and flows, expressed in Gigatonnes (1 000 million tonnes) of carbon.
The arrows are proportionate to the volume of carbon.
The figures for the flows express amounts exchanged annually.

Speed of exchange process
⟹ Very fast (less than a year)
⟹ Fast (1 to 10 years)
⟹ Slow (10 to 100 years)
⟹ Very slow (more than 100 years)

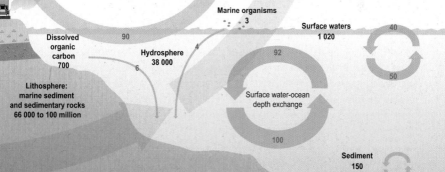

92

Ocean-atmosphere
exchange

Marine organisms
3

Surface waters
1 020

40

Dissolved
organic
carbon
700

90

Hydrosphere
38 000

4

92

50

6

Lithosphere:
marine sediment
and sedimentary rocks
66 000 to 100 million

Surface water-ocean
depth exchange

100

Sediment
150

Three – protecting human health

Emissions linked to the burning of fossil fuels' – e.g. sulfur oxides (SO_x) and nitrogen oxides (NO_x) – often help to make people ill, or even to kill them. Air pollution cuts 8.6 months off the life of the average European, causing 310 000 of the continent's people to die before their time every year. World-wide three million people a year die because of outdoor air pollution, the World Health Organization says. Normally healthy people may not notice what polluted air is doing to them, but those affected by lung disease or heart problems probably will. The pollution is pervasive: it comes from vehicles, power stations and factories. It also damages the natural world, through acid rain and smog. The marathon runner Haile Gebreselassie refused to compete in the 2008 Olympics because he said Beijing's pollution – all fossil-fuel related – was too dangerous for his health.

Four – boosting the economy

Individuals who reduce their energy consumption and thus their climate impact also save money. On a more macro-economic level, economic op-portunities arise from measures taken to reduce GHGs: insulating build-ings for example will not only save energy costs, but also give the building sector an enormous boost and create employment. While some sectors might suffer increased costs, many will seize the opportunity to innovate and get a step ahead of their competitors in adapting to changed market conditions.

Mitigating climate change addresses all these factors – directly or indirectly

Of all the reasons to try to reduce our climate footprint, the prospect of cli-mate change is definitely the most pressing, because it will cause the most far-reaching changes, to humans directly, but also to all the ecosystems on which we depend for our well-being. The IPCC's Fourth Assessment Re-port, released in 2007, describes in detail various emission scenarios and the associated impacts of temperature rise.

One of the IPCC's conclusions was that warming caused by human ac-tivities could lead to "abrupt or irreversible" impacts. Scientists warn that

Manufacturing a cell phone **60** **112** Using a cellphone for a year

climate change may not be a smooth linear process of a world warming gradually and steadily, but rather a series of sudden jolts, like the flips from one stable climate to another, radically different. Ice cores show this happened in the distant past, sometimes in the space of a single decade. The climate can alter very fast; many climatologists say the pace of change is already much faster than they expected ten years ago.

In that perspective, climate change is every bit as alarming as any of the threats facing humanity, and probably more alarming than most, because – without drastic change – its impacts appear certain.

So climate change and its effects matter fundamentally to everyone: what is at issue is not comfort, or lifestyle, but survival. Food security is at stake, climate refugees might hamper political security, and more uncomfortable changes will put humanity under strain. Scientists have never tried to hide the reality their research has uncovered. The danger threatening the Earth has never been a closely-guarded secret. They have tried consistently to get their message across in every way possible, including the use of the mass media.

For a long time, although the message was as clear as it could be, the audience remained unreceptive. But gradually the efforts to disseminate the warnings of science are beginning to pay off. The apathy and outright resistance are starting to crumble, and the climatologists' message is getting through to many people. Ever since the IPCC was established in 1988, the evidence of human induced climate change has grown stronger. Today IPCC says it is a 90 per cent probability of humans being responsible for most of the increase in global temperatures, and that global warming is happening faster than was predicted in the first reports.

That is the start of the change the planet needs.

Tackling climate change: mitigation and adaptation

Reducing our GHG emissions means attempting climate change *mitigation*, trying to reduce the impact we must expect. This will include new policies, innovative technologies and a change in lifestyle for all of us, all of which will certainly come **at a price**. We also need to go flat out at the

> *In his report on the economics of climate change, the development economist and former chief economist at the World Bank, Nicolas Stern, calculated the cost of keeping CO_2e concentrations below a 550 ppm threshold at around 1 per cent of global GDP by 2050. But if we do not act, he says, the overall costs and risks of climate change will be equivalent to losing at least 5 per cent of global GDP each year, now and permanently. If a wider range of risks and impacts is taken into account, the estimates of damage could rise to 20 per cent of GDP or more. The IPCC calculated the macroeconomic cost in 2030 at less than 3 per cent for stabilizing the CO_2e in the atmosphere between 445 and 535 ppm and the 2008 UNDP Human Development Report estimates that the cost of limiting temperature rise to 2°C could be less than 1.6 per cent of global GDP up till 2030. These estimates, whichever is more accurate, are significant. But with total global military spending at around 2.5 per cent of global GDP, they are far from prohibitive.*

same time on a quite different strategy, **climate adaptation**, preparing to

> *"Adaptation actions are taken to cope with a changing climate, e.g. increasing rainfall, higher temperatures, scarcer water resources or more frequent storms, at present or anticipating such changes in future. Adaptation aims at reducing the risk and damage from current and future harmful impacts cost-effectively or exploiting potential benefits. Examples of actions include using scarce water more efficiently, adapting existing building codes to withstand future climate conditions and extreme weather events, construction of flood walls and raising levels of dykes against sea level rise, development of drought-tolerant crops, selection of forestry species and practices less vulnerable to storms and fires, development of spatial plans and corridors to help species migrate." (this definition is taken from the European Commission's Green Paper – Adapting to climate change in Europe – options for EU action, SEC(2007)849)*

cope with the inevitable changes ahead (inevitable because of the inertia locked up in the atmosphere and the oceans: much of the warming we are experiencing today was caused by GHGs emitted several decades ago). Climate neutrality is a way to mitigation which will help to reduce the likely damage. This will, in turn, lessen the need for adaptation and alleviate the cost of adapting. Adaptation and mitigation can complement each other and together can significantly reduce the consequences of anthropogenic climate change – change caused by **human activities**.

> Most greenhouse gases have both natural and man-made sources. There are many natural processes that release and store GHGs, for example volcanic activity and swamps which account for considerable amounts of GHG emissions. Their concentration in the atmosphere consequently also varied in pre-industrial times. But today atmospheric concentrations of CO_2 and CH_4 far exceed the natural range over the last 650,000 years. It is clear that these enormous amounts of GHG are closely linked to human activities, such as fossil fuel combustion and land-use change, that release GHGs into the atmosphere. Nature is not capable of balancing this development.

Fat versus thin?

Who, then, needs to kick the habit and go on a climate diet? For now the answer is simple, whatever complexities may lie ahead. Equitable access to affordable energy is a priority if there is to be sustainable development. This guide is for everyone who has access to energy, and who has the possibility to use it more sustainably and responsibly than at present. That probably means most of us.

Some will argue that kicking the habit only applies to developed countries. After all, they bear a historic responsibility for most of the GHGs emitted so far. Developing countries, by contrast, have until recently depended far more on agriculture. (But this too, along with land use change – deforestation and growing crops on peat bogs – and forestry contributes to climate change.) Needless to say, much of this agricultural produce is exported – yet again – to consumers in the developed world with their insatiable appetites.

Using a diet analogy, some would say it is only the fat who can afford to diet. The thin have no surplus to shed, and would only damage themselves if they made the attempt. That is true – up to a point. But there are of course rich, climate-profligate people and organizations in the developing world, for example multinational corporations, who can make an effort to improve themselves.

The diet is certainly for them. Some developing country emissions result from rich countries' dependence on imports. Many of them produce goods or provide services from which developed countries benefit. Climate neutrality is for them too. On the other hand, there are those who live in energy poverty in richer countries who may not need to cut their emissions at all.

But that leaves a wider point unexplored: should people who are already climate-thin have the opportunity to get fatter before having to slim down to an ideal size? Or could they achieve the lifestyle they want without having

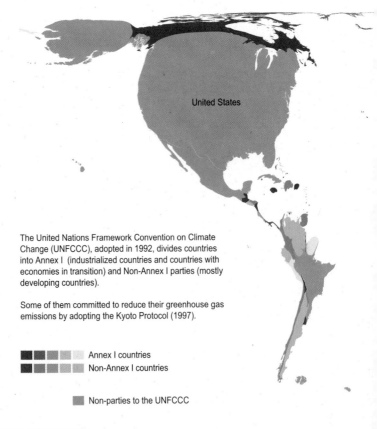

United States

The United Nations Framework Convention on Climate Change (UNFCCC), adopted in 1992, divides countries into Annex I (industrialized countries and countries with economies in transition) and Non-Annex I parties (mostly developing countries).

Some of them committed to reduce their greenhouse gas emissions by adopting the Kyoto Protocol (1997).

Annex I countries
Non-Annex I countries

Non-parties to the UNFCCC

to put on much GHG weight at all? And if they do get fatter, does that mean those who are already fat agreeing to become thinner? Not many politicians campaign on a platform of telling electors they can look forward to fewer of the good things in life. The argument goes beyond the strict question of climate change, in the sense that it embraces the whole range of resources modern society demands. But in another sense it is still about greenhouse gases, because energy is what makes things happen – just about everything that does happen.

Total CO$_2$ emissions
from fossil-fuel burning, cement production and gas flaring

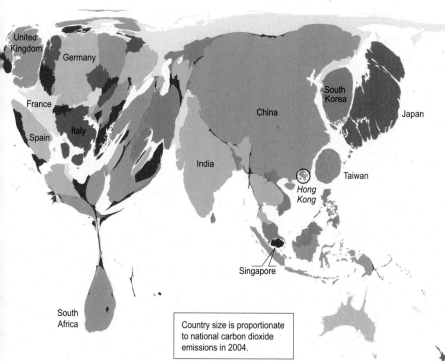

Country size is proportionate to national carbon dioxide emissions in 2004.

Cartography: SASI Group, University of Sheffield; Mark Newman, University of Michigan, 2006 (updated in 2008), www.worldmapper.org.
Data source: Gregg Marland, Tom Boden, Bob Andres, Oak Ridge National Laboratory. Please note that data for Norway is inaccurate.

Who is responsible?

Individual responsibility for climate change mitigation decreases with decreasing economic power. In poor countries more responsibility lies with those who can act, such as governments and companies.

The UN Development Programme's 2008 *Human Development Report* draws a helpful distinction between developed and developing countries. In order to stay below a global 2°C temperature rise, it suggests emissions reductions by developed countries of 80 per cent by 2050, with 30 per cent reductions by 2020. Under this scenario, developing countries would need to cut their emissions by 20 per cent by 2050, with emissions rising until 2020. Average emissions in both developed and developing countries would converge by 2060 to about 2.0 tonnes per head of CO_2e.

Another distinction is between the least-developed countries (LDCs), and the fast-developing ones, like Brazil, Russia, India and China (BRICs).

While developed countries would need to cut their emissions, some analysts suggest, the BRICs should aim to minimise their rising emissions by leapfrogging the industrialized bloc with clean technology. The LDCs would do that too, but with additional emphasis on providing support for ecosystem protection, for example by moving away from charcoal, and protecting forests and other carbon sinks. In future discussions about the share of responsibilities in reducing GHG emissions, the question of financing action will be central. The next round of negotiations for a post-Kyoto Protocol agreement will have to deal with these funding issues.

CCCC
KICK THE HABIT
THE PROBLEM

If you want to reduce **greenhouse gases**, it helps to know where on Earth

> *The greenhouse effect is an important mechanism of temperature regulation. The Earth returns energy received from the sun to space by reflecting light and emitting heat. Part of the out-going heat flow is absorbed by greenhouse gases and re-irradiated back to the Earth. Though they occur naturally, human activities have significantly increased their presence in the atmosphere. Greenhouse gases vary considerably in amounts emitted, but also in their warming effect and in the length of time they remain in the atmosphere as active warming agents.*

they come from. So what are some of the obvious ways of emitting GHGs that we may all be involved in, probably without even realising it? Here are some of the really glaring ones.

Energy for...

Energy is involved in just about everything we do. Depending on the **source**

> *Energy generation is the single most important activity resulting in GHG emissions, in particular because most of it is produced from fossil fuels such as oil, gas and coal, the latter being mainly used to generate electricity. Coal, particularly brown coal (also called lignite), is the energy source with the highest GHG emissions per energy unit. Burning coal generates 70 per cent more CO_2 than natural gas for every unit of energy. At the same time, coal is cheap and is the most widely available fossil fuel. According to the World Coal Institute, it is present in almost every country, with commercial mining in over 50. It is also the fossil fuel with the longest predicted availability. At current production levels coal will be available for at least 155 more years (compared with 41 years for oil and 65 for gas).*
>
> *But current production levels will not remain static. While coal use is falling in Western Europe it is rising in Asia and the United States. The Asia-Pacific region will be the main coal market – with 58 per cent of global coal consumption by 2025 – if current trends continue. The region is home to the largest consumer (China), the largest exporter (Australia) and the largest importer (Japan) of coal globally.*
>
> *International commitments, the progress of new technologies such as Carbon Capture and Storage (CCS, see page 88) and increased efficiency of power grids, industrial processes and so on are all ways to reduce coal-related GHG emissions. But ultimately the challenge is to develop a clean, widely available and affordable alternative to satisfy the world's energy needs (see page 144).*

of the energy, the efficiency of its use and the waste created in the process, its use and production emits from zero to enormous amounts of GHGs.

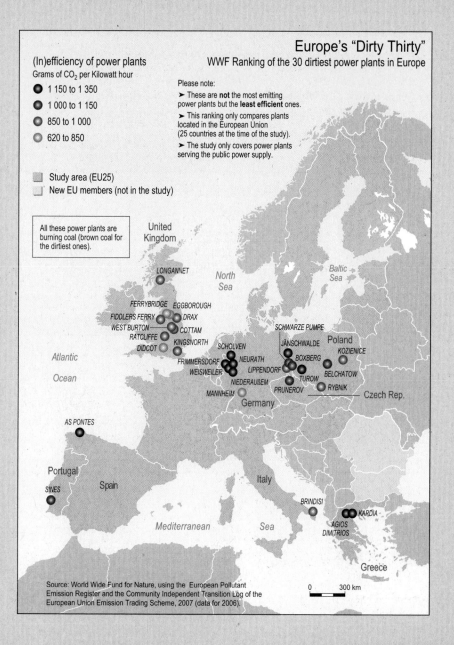

Europe's "Dirty Thirty"
WWF Ranking of the 30 dirtiest power plants in Europe

(In)efficiency of power plants
Grams of CO_2 per Kilowatt hour

- 1 150 to 1 350
- 1 000 to 1 150
- 850 to 1 000
- 620 to 850

Study area (EU25)

New EU members (not in the study)

Please note:
➤ These are **not** the most emitting power plants but the **least efficient** ones.
➤ This ranking only compares plants located in the European Union (25 countries at the time of the study).
➤ The study only covers power plants serving the public power supply.

All these power plants are burning coal (brown coal for the dirtiest ones).

United Kingdom

North Sea

Baltic Sea

LONGANNET

FERRYBRIDGE EGGBOROUGH
FIDDLERS FERRY DRAX
WEST BURTON COTTAM
RATCLIFFE KINGSNORTH
DIDCOT

SCHWARZE PUMPE

SCHOLVEN
JÄNSCHWALDE KOZIENICE
Poland
BOXBERG

FRIMMERSDORF NEURATH
WEISWEILER LIPPENDORF BELCHATOW
NIEDERAUßEM TUROW
MANNHEIM PRUNEROV RYBNIK
Germany Czech Rep.

Atlantic Ocean

AS PONTES

Portugal

SINES Spain Italy

Mediterranean Sea

BRINDISI KARDIA
AGIOS DIMITRIOS

Greece

Source: World Wide Fund for Nature, using the European Pollutant Emission Register and the Community Independent Transition Log of the European Union Emission Trading Scheme, 2007 (data for 2006).

0   300 km

Greenhouse gas emissions for three sectors

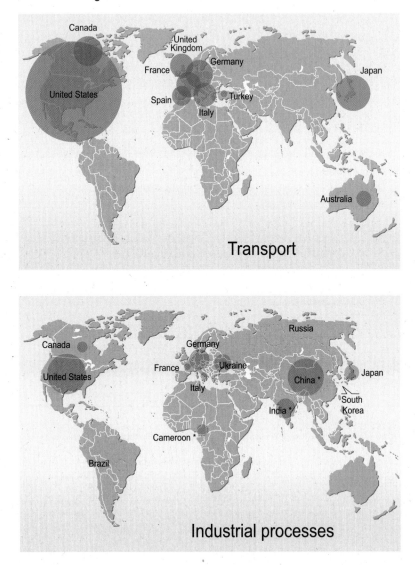

Transport

Industrial processes

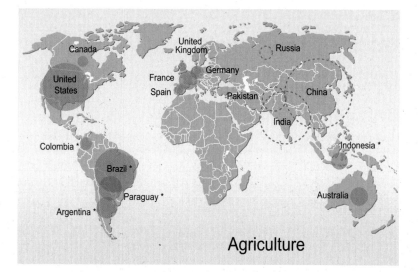

Agriculture

The data comes from national reports to UNFCCC.
For developing countries (i. e. non-Annex I countries), data is either old or missing.
To better reflect the truth, we chose to overlap 2000 data from IEA (dashed circles).
Please note that the calculation methods are different.

Data is for 2004, except * (1994) and dashed circles (2000).

Only emissions above 40 million tonnes
of CO_2 equivalent are represented.

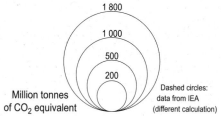

1 800
1 000
500
200

Million tonnes
of CO_2 equivalent

Dashed circles:
data from IEA
(different calculation)

Sources: UNFCCC, 2007; International Energy Agency, 2004.

...Production and consumption

Since 1987 the Earth's population has grown by almost 30 per cent, and global economic output has risen by 76 per cent. Average per capita gross national income has almost doubled, from about US$3 300 to US$6 400. And just about everything needs energy to be produced. The global primary energy supply (80 per cent of it supplied by fossil fuels) increased by 4 per cent annually from 1987 to 2004. Demand for energy is predicted to continue to grow by at least 50 per cent by 2030, as the fast-developing countries like Brazil, Russia, India and China continue their rapid economic growth. For China, a recent analysis by economists at the University of California, Berkeley, and University of California, San Diego, showed that the annual emissions growth rate for China will be at least 11 per cent for the period between 2004 and 2010. However it should be borne in mind that with about 4 tonnes of CO_2 per capita, China still emits half as much as Spain, and only a fifth as much as an average US citizen.

Almost everything we produce and consume means GHG emissions today, because we do not use much renewable energy or live very sustainably. Much of what we use may arrive with superfluous **packaging**, itself

Aluminium for example is a highly energy-intensive product. The production of one kilo of aluminium requires about 14 kWh of electricity. In practical terms that means that with the energy needed to produce 1 metre of standard aluminium foil, you could light your kitchen with a regular light bulb (60 W) for more than two hours or with an energy-saving bulb (11 W) for about 13 hours. Recycled aluminium requires only about 5 per cent of the energy needed to produce new aluminium.

a problem to dispose of, a waste of energy and a source of emissions. And much of what is bought ends up being thrown away sooner or later. Waste rots away, emitting methane if it is organic, or emitting CO_2 if it is burned. Waste and waste water accounts for about 3 per cent of human-induced GHG emissions.

... Transport

But not only consuming ever more goods demands a lot of energy. Getting from one place to another does, too. Most of us value transport – or perhaps we do not value it as highly as we should, assuming instead that

Share of transport-related
greenhouse gas emissions

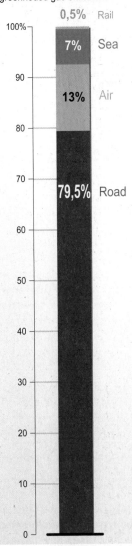

Varying contribution
to climate change

Source: *Evaluation des politiques publiques au regard des changements climatiques*, Climate Action Network (RAC), French Environmental and Energy Management Agency (Ademe), December 2005.

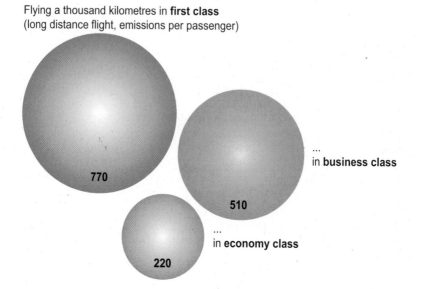

Flying a thousand kilometres in **first class**
(long distance flight, emissions per passenger)

770

...
in **business class**

510

...
in **economy class**

220

it is our right. Personal and commercial transport consumes about 20 per cent of the global energy supply, 80 per cent of which comes from fossil fuels. So the more an individual acquires or consumes commodities that have had to travel to the point of use, the larger their climate footprint will be. Globally, the energy used by   ***road transport***   is the biggest chunk in

New cars are becoming more and more efficient, but this trend is counterbalanced with more miles driven and more vehicles on the road. According to the World Resources Institute global vehicle production increased about 14 per cent between 1999 and 2005. In India Tata Motors launched the world's cheapest car, the Tata Nano, at the beginning of 2008. It will sell for 100 000 rupees, or US$2 500. Nanos will replace many highly-polluting two-stroke vehicles. And their owners have as much right to drive as anyone else. Tata will start by making about 250 000 Nanos and expects annual demand eventually to reach 1 million cars, to add to the 13 million or so on the country's roads already. On the other hand, experts say India's greenhouse gas emissions will rise almost seven-fold if car travel remains unchecked.

transport-related emissions, accounting for more than 70 per cent within the sector. Road transport saw an emissions increase of 46.5 per cent between 1987 and 2004. Air travel is expanding fast: the miles flown rose between

How much is emitted by ships?

2007 estimates

1 210 ▮ Million tons of CO$_2$

1996 estimates

437

800

Source: *Study of Greenhouse Gas Emissions from Ships, Final Report to the International Maritime Organization, March 2000.*

Sources: Inputs from the International Maritime Organization (IMO); John Vidal, "*Shipping boom fuels rising tide of global CO2 emissions*", The Guardian, 13 February 2008; www.oceana.org/climate.

1990 and 2003 by 80 per cent. According to an unpublished report by the International Maritime Organisation, shipping emitted around 800 million tonnes of CO$_2$ in 2007, which amounts to almost three per cent of global emissions. This means shipping related CO$_2$ emissions have almost doubled over the past ten years. Other sources are indicating even higher figures, up to 1210 million tonnes or nearly 4.5 per cent of global CO$_2$ emissions.

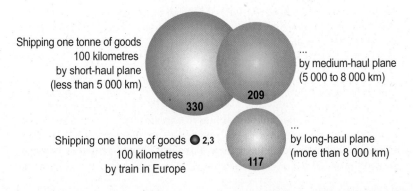

Shipping one tonne of goods 100 kilometres by short-haul plane (less than 5 000 km)

... by medium-haul plane (5 000 to 8 000 km)

330

209

Shipping one tonne of goods 100 kilometres by train in Europe ● 2,3

... by long-haul plane (more than 8 000 km)

117

... and Housing

Buildings are responsible for more than 40 per cent of energy use in OECD countries and at a global level they account for about 30 per cent of GHG emissions according to UNEP's Sustainable Building and Construction Initiative. In absolute terms the amount is rising fast as construction continues apace, especially in rapidly developing countries. Heating, cooling and lighting our homes and using household appliances absorbs 11 per cent of global energy. Yet the average UK household could save around two tonnes of CO_2 annually by making its home *energy-efficient*; in essence, improve

The World Business Council for Sustainable Development's Energy Efficiency in Buildings (EEB) project concludes that by cutting energy use in buildings by about 30 per cent, Europe's energy consumption would fall by 11 per cent, more than half of the 20-20-20 target (20 per cent less carbon dioxide by 2020, with 20 per cent renewables in the energy mix). What is more, it saves money.

insulation, heating systems and lighting.

Construction in itself affects GHG emissions. **Cement** for example is a

The cement industry contributes about 5 per cent to global anthropogenic CO_2 emissions, making it an important target for CO_2 emission mitigation strategies. Whereas concrete can be recycled by crushing it and using it to replace gravel in road construction, cement has no viable recycling potential; each new road and building needs new cement. In booming economies from Asia to Eastern Europe new construction is both a driver and a consequence of increasing wealth, which is also why about 80 per cent of all cement is made and used in emerging economies.

high-emission construction material, whereas wood is renewable and thus climate-friendly. But be careful: there's good wood and not-so-good wood. If a forest has to be cut down to build your house and is not re-established afterwards, additional CO_2 will be emitted, just as with concrete (that goes for furniture as well).

Agriculture

Agriculture is an important contributor to climate change with GHG emissions comparable in volume to the transport sector. First, there is the carbon emitted from tilling and deforestation. Then there is the use of fossil fuels in fertiliser production and other agricultural chemicals, for farm machinery in

Average emissions
Thousand million tonnes of CO$_2$ equivalent per year

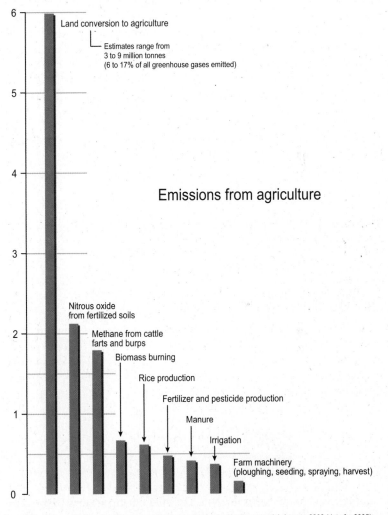

Land conversion to agriculture

Estimates range from
3 to 9 million tonnes
(6 to 17% of all greenhouse gases emitted)

Emissions from agriculture

Nitrous oxide
from fertilized soils

Methane from cattle
farts and burps

Biomass burning

Rice production

Fertilizer and pesticide production

Manure

Irrigation

Farm machinery
(ploughing, seeding, spraying, harvest)

Source: Greenpeace, *Cool farming: Climate impacts of agriculture and mitigation potential*, January 2008 (data for 2005).

Dirty coal is here to stay

Main production basins

Brown coal *

Hard coal **

Major consumers in red

Coal producers are already taking advantage of the oil shortage and might even more in the future.

The end of the oil era

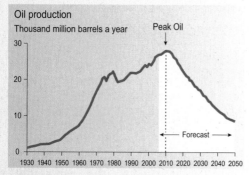

Oil production
Thousand million barrels a year

Peak Oil

30

20

10

0

1930 1940 1950 1960 1970 1980 1990 2000 2010 2020 2030 2040 2050

← Forecast →

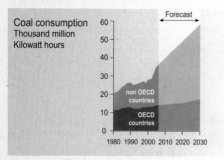

Coal consumption
Thousand million
Kilowatt hours

Forecast

60
50
40
30
20
10
0

non OECD
countries

OECD
countries

1980 1990 2000 2010 2020 2030

North America

UNITED
STATES

ATLANTIC
OCEAN

South and Central America

* Lignite and sub-bituminous coal (the dirtiest)
** Anthracite and bituminous coal (coking coal and steam coal)

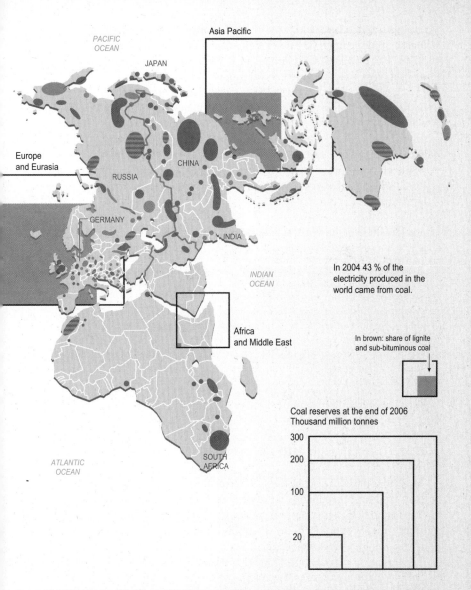

Asia Pacific

PACIFIC
OCEAN

JAPAN

Europe
and Eurasia

RUSSIA

CHINA

GERMANY

INDIA

INDIAN
OCEAN

Africa
and Middle East

In 2004 43 % of the
electricity produced in the
world came from coal.

In brown: share of lignite
and sub-bituminous coal

ATLANTIC
OCEAN

SOUTH
AFRICA

Coal reserves at the end of 2006
Thousand million tonnes

300

200

100

20

Sources: BP Statistical Review of World Energy 2007; US Department of Energy Information Administration (EIA), International Energy
Annual 2004, 2006; EIA, System for the Analysis of Global Energy Markets, 2007; World Energy Council, Survey of Energy Resources 2004;
Coaltrans World Coal Map 2005; International Energy Agency; OECD Glossary of Statistical Terms, 2008; Atlas Environnement du Monde
Diplomatique 2007; Colin Campbell, Association for the study of peak oil and gas, 2007.

intensive agriculture, and for transporting animals and crops from farm to market. But the main GHGs emitted in agriculture are methane and nitrous oxide, which underlines the need to become climate and not just carbon-neutral. This is mainly due to meat production.

Cattle, water buffalo, sheep and other ruminants are animals with a special stomach that allows them to digest tough plant material. Digestion produces methane, which the animals get rid of by releasing it at either end. Nitrous oxide release is mostly linked to the use of artificial nitrate fertilizers to improve yields. Nitrogen fertilizer in particular is extremely fossil fuel-intensive, requiring 1.5 tonnes of oil equivalents to make 1 tonne of fertilizer.

A 2006 study of the impacts of the **food production chain** across the Euro-

If you do a life-cycle analysis of the food chain you must factor in agricultural production, manufacturing, refrigeration, transport, packaging, retail, home storage, cooking and waste disposal. Different foods cause impacts at different stages. Potatoes, chickpeas and tea leaves, for example, need fewer greenhouse gases to grow than they do to cook – baking a potato in an oven, boiling chickpeas for an hour till soft, or switching the kettle on for tea all consume significant amounts of energy. For frozen vegetables refrigeration is the key emission stage. Considering all these factors and obtaining all the necessary information to do so may be a difficult task, therefore doing a qualitative assessment can sometimes be a good alternative and the more practical solution.

pean Union found it accounted for 31 per cent of all EU GHG emissions.

Land use change and deforestation

Another important part of the CO_2 in the atmosphere comes from changes in land use, responsible for almost 20 per cent of atmospheric carbon. Trees and other plants remove carbon from the atmosphere in the process of growing. When they decay or are burnt, much of this stored carbon escapes back into the atmosphere.

Deforestation also causes the release of the carbon stored in the soil (as does ploughing), and if the forest is not restored afterwards the land will store much less CO_2.

Annual methane emissions from the farts and burps of a **cow**

... of a **pig**
230

... of an **ox**

... of a **goat**
370

1 740

3 500

... of a **sheep**

320

Increasing numbers of livestock in modern energy intensive farming systems are given high-energy feed like soya, often produced in developing countries (and often used in developed ones). To find the land to grow it ranchers will sometimes turn forests to pasture. So our meal of choice has direct consequences for the climate. A report by the UN's Food and Agriculture Organization found that, globally, livestock accounts for 18 per cent of GHG emissions (37 per cent of human-related global methane and 65 per cent of global nitrous oxide emissions), a figure that includes deforestation to clear land for animals, and associated emissions.

Agriculture is only one of the reasons for deforestation. Activities that result in land disturbance such as opencast mining or the building of sprawling cities are other pressures on virgin forests. Destruction of wetlands and peat bogs also destroys carbon sinks.

World Greenhouse gas emissions by sector

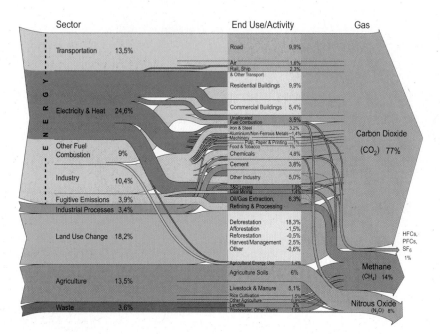

Sector | End Use/Activity | Gas

Transportation 13,5%
- Road 9,9%
- Air 1,6%
- Rail, Ship & Other Transport 2,3%

Electricity & Heat 24,6%
- Residential Buildings 9,9%
- Commercial Buildings 5,4%
- Unallocated Fuel Combustion 3,5%

Other Fuel Combustion 9%
- Iron & Steel 3,2%
- Aluminium/Non-Ferrous Metals 1,4%
- Machinery 1%
- Pulp, Paper & Printing 1%
- Food & Tobacco 1%

Industry 10,4%
- Chemicals 4,8%
- Cement 3,8%
- Other Industry 5,0%
- T&D Losses 1,9%
- Coal Mining 1,4%

Fugitive Emissions 3,9%
Industrial Processes 3,4%
- Oil/Gas Extraction, Refining & Processing 6,3%

Land Use Change 18,2%
- Deforestation 18,3%
- Afforestation -1,5%
- Reforestation -0,5%
- Harvest/Management 2,5%
- Other -0,6%

Agriculture 13,5%
- Agricultural Energy Use 1,4%
- Agriculture Soils 6%
- Livestock & Manure 5,1%
- Rice Cultivation 1,5%
- Other Agriculture 0,9%

Waste 3,6%
- Landfills 2%
- Wastewater, Other Waste 1,6%

Carbon Dioxide (CO$_2$) 77%
HFCs, PFCs, SF$_6$ 1%
Methane (CH$_4$) 14%
Nitrous Oxide (N$_2$O) 8%

All data is for 2000. All calculations are based on CO$_2$ equivalents, using 100-year global warming potentials from the IPCC (1996), based on a total global estimate of 41 755 MtCO$_2$ equivalent. Land use change includes both emissions and absorptions. Dotted lines represent flows of less than 0.1% percent of total GHG emissions.

Source: World Resources Institute, Climate Analysis Indicator Tool (CAIT), Navigating the Numbers: Greenhouse Gas Data and International Climate Policy, December 2005; Intergovernmental Panel on Climate Change, 1996 (data for 2000).

CCCC

KICK THE HABIT

THE ACTORS

So there is a problem, it is urgent, and it affects almost every part of life. Something must be done. But what? And who should do it? Politicians? Absolutely. Business and industry? Certainly. Science and technology? Obviously. The United Nations? Of course. But if we really do want a changed world, it is useful to remember where to begin: be the change you want to see. It comes down to each one of us. No individual is going to make a scrap of difference. But millions of individuals together can make all the difference. The gulf yawns before us, but no one is going to try to cross it in a single leap. Doing the impossible involves starting from where we are, as a way to prompting action by those who can make a real difference, such as governments.

Speaking at the UN Bali climate conference in December 2007 the UNEP executive director, Achim Steiner, said: "The science, but also increasingly the day-to-day experience of millions of people, tells us climate change is a reality. Addressing it is an opportunity we cannot fail to take. So why not address it now? And if not here, where? If not now, when?"

There is plenty of advice available about how to become climate-neutral. What this book aims to do is point you to some of the sources and guides that will be most useful to you. It contains pointers for individuals; small and large organizations; cities; and countries. Obviously these are not separate, watertight categories.

● INDIVIDUALS

Individual commitment is critical. All social groups consist of individuals: we are responsible for the choices we make. But we also live in cities, belong to NGOs, may work for a small or a large organization, and are citizens of our countries, with more or less democratic power to influence national politics. Therefore we have to accept the fact of our responsibility in each of these different spheres and act to empower ourselves and others. It sounds a tall order in an age when for many personal satisfaction and fulfilment is all that counts. But is it so different from accepting the responsibility of looking after one's health?

As individuals, we are responsible for GHGs we emit directly through our daily actions – the way we live, the way we move around and what and how we consume. But we also *indirectly* influence what is emitted by making

Some might use the argument that whatever they do as individuals is too little to affect the planet, so they need not bother to make an effort. These people are maybe not aware that even if not directly emitting, their way of life has an indirect influence over GHG emissions, and that, albeit indirectly, with their influence things might change "out there". If you break down for instance a typical western European's GHG emissions to individual shares, less than 50 per cent are direct emissions (such as driving a car or using a heater) while the rest are indirect – and individuals have no direct control over them. 20 per cent are caused by the products we consume and the emissions that have arisen in producing and disposing of them, 25 per cent come from powering workplaces, and 10 per cent from maintaining public infrastructure. Financial institutions for example have relatively small GHG emissions in proportion to their size. Reducing their travel or building-related emissions is a good idea. But they could exert much greater influence over the projects they lend to, requiring them to be climate-friendly.

choices that are more or less climate-relevant – what kind of products we buy, which politicians we support, what kind of stocks we invest in, to name just a few examples. We might not be as aware of our indirect responsibility as of our direct influence, but by giving it some thought we might be able to achieve just as much in reducing GHG emissions by influencing those indirect paths as by reducing our own, direct emissions.

SMALL ORGANIZATIONS

Small and medium enterprises *(SMEs)* and non-governmental organiza-

The Worldwatch Institute argues for GHG reduction strategies for companies: "... And there's money in minimizing energy use. Research in one industrialized country shows that a lack of time and expertise to measure and reduce carbon emissions is preventing small and medium businesses from saving as much energy as they could. Many underestimate the savings they could achieve: nearly 23 per cent of those studied believed their business could save only between one per cent and four per cent on energy bills, although the average figure was ten per cent. Yet one in three of the businesses that did measure their emissions said it was to gain a competitive edge, the same number also said they wanted to adapt before legislation required them to."

tions (NGOs) perform multiple roles. Just like individuals, they run their own households. They are consumers and producers; they provide goods or services; they are responsible for the property and buildings they own. In addition to that, one of their most significant responsibilities is as examples to their employees or members.

SMEs are often characterized by a strong personal leader figure. They operate mainly in a regional context, rarely across national borders. Their products may well be intermediate inputs for the production of goods by bigger companies. At the same time, they depend on raw materials. They have little or no influence on the way these inputs are produced or exploited.

Suppose for instance that you are running a business that uses precious metals in its process, or its products. You will have to depend on the work of the people who mine the metals – and they may be obliged to destroy a forest to reach their goal and earn a living. Or again, palm oil is used in a huge range of products, from soap to margarine, and now increasingly in biofuels. Growing it can mean forest destruction and consequent releases of CO_2 and methane, and probably other GHGs.

But business can influence emissions through its policies. If your procurement policy, for example, depends on spare parts or raw materials reaching

Producing and managing the end-of-life of one tonne of cardboard packaging (without printing)

Producing and managing the end-of-life of one tonne of bottle glass packaging

1990   **455**

your plant "just in time", it saves you the cost of extra storage space. But it may mean more individual journeys to keep the production lines running. If you want to avoid the cost of designing buildings with "thinking" heating and ventilation systems, you may conclude that it will be best just to heat the building to a comfortable temperature and leave the workers to open the windows when they get too hot (this was the standard industrial model across much of the former Soviet bloc, and almost certainly persists in places there – and elsewhere).

NGOs working for the public interest, as many do, may think they are exempt from climate accountability. What matters is to think through the implications of everything you buy or do. And both NGOs and business set a significant example to their workers, customers and supporters. Humanitarian groups also need to include climate protection in their operations, and most already do so. Most of those who will be affected worst and soonest by climate change are among the poorest of the poor.

LARGE ORGANIZATIONS

Corporations, multinationals and intergovernmental organizations are in most ways similar to SMEs and NGOs, except that their possibilities for damaging or protecting the climate are correspondingly greater. Their size means they have more influence, however they choose to wield it. Both categories can exert more pressure on their employees and members than public administrations and politicians, because most of them are organized in a hierarchical way. Despite this, they are part of political systems with which they have to comply. This is where governments can bring their influence to bear. There are clear differences between sectors. Heavy industry, for example, produces high direct emissions, which a bank will not do. But it might have the same degree of responsibility, because of the way it devises and implements its loans policy.

Companies that buy materials or products from suppliers who themselves are responsible for large emissions are missing a good opportunity to use their power and size for good. They can site their offices or factories in the countries where they want to have them – for profit, efficiency or any other reason. So they may be open to the temptation to suit their own convenience without thinking of anything else. And, like small and medium enterprises, they want equal treatment: they do not want to be disadvantaged by a sterner regime than their competitors face. They demand a global emissions reduction regime, monitored and enforced locally.

The corporate responsibility message is now widely accepted by most leading companies, not only because they know they may be punished by their customers if they do not appear to be trying hard to be green but also because it is **profitable.** A green business outlook is more than simply

For most corporate decision makers, the central question narrows to whether their decisions optimize share value. The evidence suggests that higher levels of corporate social responsibility are associated with higher share values. A report released in July 2007 by Goldman Sachs, one of the world's leading investment banks, showed that in the six sectors covered – energy, mining, steel, food, beverages, and media – companies that are considered leaders in implementing environmental, social and governance policies created have sustained competitive advantage and outperformed the general stock market by 25 per cent since August 2005. Moreover 72 per cent of these companies outperformed their peers in the same industries over the same period.

cosmetic. A bank, for example, may be a model enterprise in terms of its procurement, premises and travel policies. But its lending policy may involve it in supporting customers who could make massive improvements in protecting the atmosphere. What is needed to persuade them to do so is a nudge and who better than a bank to deliver it?

For inter-governmental organizations there can be a temptation to think you are so important that you are above the law – even the physical law which says CO_2 levels are approaching danger level. Their close interchanges across the globe imply a lot of travelling – sometimes not necessarily linked to the result of the mission.

 CITIES

Cities are themselves sources of global warming: they are "heat islands", significantly warmer than the surrounding countryside. The main reason for this is the way the land surface is modified by urban development; waste heat from energy use is a secondary cause.

If cities have an advantage in working towards climate neutrality it probably lies in their closeness to their citizens. Many people identify closely with the city where they were born or where they live, which is why local politics and local news media are often far more interesting to many people than what happens on the national stage. Local governments add to atmospheric damage when they design city centres to suit vehicles, not pedestrians, and when they design buildings to the cheapest and not the highest standards. They do so by ignoring their own environmental footprint, the huge swathe of surrounding countryside from which they absorb many resources, resources they could often find within their own limits, obviating the need for transport. They do so by giving low or no priority to recycling and waste disposal policies.

COUNTRIES

National governments have a key role to play in working towards climate neutrality. They can apply various instruments that can change people's behaviour. Legislation and economic incentives, used in the right mix, will make a great difference. Twenty years ago many governments acted to reduce and then eliminate the use of ozone-destroying CFCs. There were protests, but it happened. Today, however, a few governments are markedly reluctant to give a similar lead to cutting damaging climate emissions. This leaves business and industry confused or unable to act, for fear of losing markets to less scrupulous competitors. It also leaves individual citizens unconvinced that climate change really is a problem at all: if it mattered, they argue, then surely the government would do something about it. And beyond the domestic agenda governments have the option to downplay, or not, the urgency of what is happening.

Top 20 greenhouse gas emitters
(including land use change and forestry)

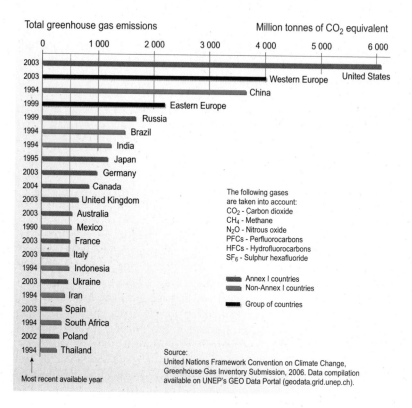

Total greenhouse gas emissions

Million tonnes of CO_2 equivalent

| | 0 | 1 000 | 2 000 | 3 000 | 4 000 | 5 000 | 6 000 |

2003 — United States
2003 — Western Europe
1994 — China
1999 — Eastern Europe
1999 — Russia
1994 — Brazil
1994 — India
1995 — Japan
2003 — Germany
2004 — Canada
2003 — United Kingdom
2003 — Australia
1990 — Mexico
2003 — France
2003 — Italy
1994 — Indonesia
2003 — Ukraine
1994 — Iran
2003 — Spain
1994 — South Africa
2002 — Poland
1994 — Thailand

↑ Most recent available year

The following gases
are taken into account:
CO_2 - Carbon dioxide
CH_4 - Methane
N_2O - Nitrous oxide
PFCs - Perfluorocarbons
HFCs - Hydrofluorocarbons
SF_6 - Sulphur hexafluoride

▬▬ Annex I countries
▬▬ Non-Annex I countries
▬▬ Group of countries

Source:
United Nations Framework Convention on Climate Change,
Greenhouse Gas Inventory Submission, 2006. Data compilation
available on UNEP's GEO Data Portal (geodata.grid.unep.ch).

CCCC

KICK THE HABIT

THE REDUCTION CYCLE

COUNT AND ANALYSE   ACT   REDUCE   OFFSET   EVALUATE

The key to success for an effective emissions reduction programme is to have a well-organized, performing structure and a clear process in place. The first step is to **decide** to go climate-neutral: that obviously comes first. Then we need to **count** the GHG emissions for which we are directly responsible and **analyse** where are those emissions coming from? Then comes the need to find out what we must do to lower or stop them, what options we have, and to **act** on that knowledge. The last steps are to **evaluate** what we have done, identify flaws and then **start all over again**, hopefully taking into account the lessons learnt in the first round.

Get a firm commitment

Before any of this is going to happen, of course, someone has to take a clear decision to work to become climate neutral. It will certainly be an individual's decision, but for more complex set-ups, it will be wider than that. For it to get very far, it will need *positive political leadership* at the highest level

Norway is one of five countries to have publicly declared their intention to work towards climate neutrality (the others are Costa Rica, Iceland, Monaco and New Zealand). Norway aims to reach its goal by 2030. The decision was taken by the government under the leadership of the Prime Minister – but, crucially, it enlisted the agreement of the opposition parties as well. The Finance Minister, Kristin Halvorsen, said: "The purpose of the government parties' invitation to the opposition was to create a broad-based, long-term majority platform on which a proactive Norwegian climate policy could be based." A lot of money is going into efforts to promote renewable energy, strengthen public transport and implement measures aimed at reducing emissions from transport.

The UN is not simply telling other people how to reduce their greenhouse gas emissions, it aims to do so itself. The Secretary-General, Ban Ki-moon, says the organization is moving toward making its New York headquarters climate neutral and environmentally sustainable. The initiative should ultimately include the other UN headquarters and offices around the globe. To help make sure the "greening" effort extends across the entire UN system, the Secretary-General has asked the heads of all UN agencies, funds and programmes to join the effort through an initiative supported by the Environment Management Group (EMG).

and wide popular agreement that the effort is worth making. The Intergovernmental Panel on Climate Change, the UN Framework Convention on Climate Change and the Kyoto Protocol under the convention represent global leaders' commitment to confront the problem. The degree to which they succeed will show the depth of that commitment. The British environmental writer Crispin Tickell once spelt out his recipe for avoiding dangerous climate change: "Leadership from the top, pressure from below – and an instructive disaster." Perhaps a combination of the first two elements may spare us the need for the third.

Once the decision is taken at the highest level (of a country, city or other group) it can be invaluable to have another senior figure to champion climate neutrality, addressing senior management and workers alike. "Senior" need not mean a traditionally respectable pillar of society: the term can include anybody who is widely known and popular. Footballers and pop stars make ideal champions.

Then comes the stage of assessing the situation by counting total emissions and analysing their source – making an inventory, in other words. At least as important is to analyse the options available for reducing them. With those results it is possible to set priorities and targets. To what extent can we reduce our own emissions and how much do we have to offset? How long should it take (Norway had originally set itself a deadline of 2050 and recently moved it to 2030)? Where will policymakers get the biggest bang for their buck – where should resources and efforts be concentrated to achieve the best and most visible results? And what yardsticks will be needed to measure progress towards targets (this question is covered in more detail below)? And who will guarantee that progress really is being made?

After settling the broad principles, the next stage is to develop a detailed action plan which puts flesh on the bones of the strategic outline. This plan will include a timeframe, responsibilities, the targets to be achieved and the indicators used to gauge progress.

Implementing the plan, the moment when deliberation becomes action, comes next, and it has to be accompanied by systematic monitoring of the process. This in turn is followed by evaluation of the results and compilation of a list of suggested improvements, with results documented and reported, so that experience gained of what does (and does not) work is shared with those who can put it to good use.

Finally, with all that completed, the cycle starts all over again, only this time incorporating the lessons learnt. Science and technology move on, regulations become tighter, the standards people demand go up. So the second cycle will go further than the first, and the process will continue, each successive phase building on and improving on what went before.

It should not need saying (but possibly it does) that throughout the entire process it is vital to ensure that you speak – and listen – to everyone who has agreed to support it, in order to make sure that they continue to do so. Feeling that you are being ignored is a very effective route to losing confidence in someone else's big idea. Also, make sure you try continually to win new supporters, and explain what you are doing to the public –

ENVIRONMENTAL MANAGEMENT SYSTEMS

One potentially useful tool that businesses as well as local administration can make use of for the process of starting to work towards climate neutrality is an environmental (or sustainability) management system or EMS based on a simple principle, the Continual Improvement Cycle: **Plan – Do – Check – Act**. An EMS focuses on environmental management practices, rather than the activities themselves, so it will ensure that proper procedures are in place and training for workers exists, but it will not specify the methods to use or the frequency that a pollutant needs to be sampled or monitored.

It can assure managers that they are in control of processes and activities that impact on the environment, and confirm to employees that they are working for an environmentally responsible organization. Beyond this, it helps the company to provide assurance on environmental issues to customers, the community and regulators, and to ensure compliance with environmental regulations.

The basic EMS framework is established by the international standard ISO 14001 (developed by the International Organization for Standardization). Another EMS framework is EMAS, the European Eco Management and Audit Scheme, used by numerous companies throughout the EU. Many local tax payers are interested in where their money goes, and as consumers they want to know what the company providing their goods is doing to protect the climate. Give them the opportunity to participate too. Here it can be useful to involve the media in telling people about what you are doing.

The whole scheme will obviously need adapting to the group concerned: what works well on a country-wide scale may be rather too elaborate and complex for an SME or an NGO, for example. This organizational set-up in a cycle is closely aligned with the approach employed in environmental management systems.

authorities apply the management system to certain sectors of their administration or certify their whole operations.

A national example for an environmental certification system is the Norwegian Eco-Lighthouse Programme. Through the programme companies reduce their impact on the environment, cut costs and benefit from their status as an environmentally responsible company. The "Eco-Lighthouse" concept was born in 1996, when six municipalities were selected to participate in "Sustainable Communities," a Norwegian Local Agenda 21 pilot programme. The city authorities presented a proposal to nine companies as diverse as a hotel, a housepainter, an ice-cream factory and a wood product company. The city paid a consultant to do an environmental audit and draw up a three-year plan for reducing resource consumption and environmental impact. In return, the firms undertook to carry out the plan and share their experiences with other firms in the same industry. Based on the audits, criteria for local, industry-specific environmental certification schemes were developed.

The concept spread further and since 2006, the Norwegian capital Oslo has required Eco-Lighthouse certifica.tion from all its public enterprises, from hospitals to waste management facilities and down to kindergartens.

Count and analyse

What gets measured, gets managed

Counting and analyzing the emissions that you need to eliminate, and the options you have for doing so, is the most crucial step in the cycle, because without this knowledge you will be working in the dark. It enables you to decide the priorities for action – from the food you eat and the products you buy to energy use and transport – and to start monitoring your progress. Anyone starting on a diet will be sure to step on the scales the first day, partly to know the extent of the problem and also to have a baseline for recording their (presumed) progress towards their target weight. So you need an inventory.

The inventory aims at answering questions such as:
- Which operations, activities, units should be included?
- Which sources should be included?
- Who is responsible for which emissions?
- Which gases should be included?

Step one: Set up your inventory
Step two: Count your emissions

When making an inventory of GHG emissions, we are immediately confronted with the question of where to start, and where to end. We will probably not want to stick at accounting for our CO_2 emissions alone, but include all GHGs. There are several problems here. Carbon dioxide is the most abundant of them, but several of the others, although much rarer, are far more destructive, molecule for molecule. So we will need to be familiar with the idea of CO_2 equivalence – the impact a GHG has on the atmosphere expressed in the equivalent amount of CO_2. The US Environmental Protection Agency provides a helpful Greenhouse Gas Equivalencies Converter to translate GHGs at www.epa.gov/cleanenergy/energy-resources/calculator.html. Depending on what we want our inventory for, it will need to provide different levels of transparency and possibilities for verification. In particular if your goal is trading emissions, a standardized approach is the only way to ensure that actual emissions in one organization correspond to those in another and are offset in equal amounts.

● INDIVIDUALS

For individuals, carbon calculators simplify compiling an inventory. Typically you will need to know your electricity consumption in kWh, how much and what kind of fuel you use to heat your water and warm the house, and how many kilometres you drive, fly and ride in different vehicles. You also need to decide the limits of the system you are concerned with, whether it is you as individuals, your household, or the company you work for.

And that still leaves unsettled the range of the emissions you are prepared to acknowledge. It may be simply those for which you are directly responsible – the fumes that come out of your car's exhaust and the emissions from your central heating. But you may decide to set your bounds much wider and incorporate at least some of the gases *"embedded"* in every-

Carbon and climate labels might in future help to identify indirect emissions. Given the complicated life cycle of products, however, one may imagine how difficult it is to create an accurate label at product level, let alone compare different products with each other. A carbon label, which shows the carbon footprint inherent in putting a product on the shelf, was introduced in the UK in March 2007 by the Carbon Trust. Examples of products featuring their carbon footprint are Walkers Crisps, Innocent Drinks, and Boots shampoos.

thing you use or buy. But the more you include the more complex your task to measure the emissions will become. While you might lose in accuracy, you are more certain not to ignore a big chunk of your emissions. Probably the simplest rule is to include those emissions you control and those resulting from the products and services you pay for. It will not give you a perfect answer or even a complete one, but it will let you make a start, from which you can hope to improve your performance later. Just under half the emissions for which those individuals in developed countries are responsible come from things over which we have some control, for example how much we drive and fly and how we heat and power our homes. The rest arises indirectly from powering the places where we work, from maintaining public infrastructure and government, and during the production of the things we buy, including food. These are some of the factors that anyone will want to think about as they decide how to start their climate diet.

Calculating emissions – tools for Individuals

Online options
There are plenty of carbon calculators available online. There is also wide variation between their usefulness and capabilities. Often this is because they are measuring different parameters. Some, for example, factor in only a few possible culprits, like cars, aircraft and household energy use. Others cast their nets wider, covering household waste or leisure interests as well. Enter "climate footprint" into a well-known search engine, and it comes up with a range of answers which are possibly not exactly what you are looking for. The first, from the highly-reputable World Resources Institute turns out to be a carbon footprint calculator – not as comprehensive as you may be wanting if you are going to assess your entire GHG emissions, although it does offer you the chance to use it even if you do not live in North America. More appealing at first sight is the Lifestyle Climate Footprint Calculator from the University of California's Berkeley Institute of the Environment. But this, too, deals only in carbon dioxide, and is for US users alone. Searches for methane and nitrous oxide calculators designed for general use produce no results. So for now it is a question of starting by working out simply what your CO_2 emissions are: no doubt there will be more comprehensive calculators available soon

Beyond calculating and all over the world
Another helpful site for individuals is provided by the fossil fuel multinational BP. It covers relatively few countries, but they do include China and South Africa. You can pass your cursor over various on-screen icons and find information about ways to reduce your carbon emissions. There are three main areas: At Home, In the Store, and On the Road. The At Home info-icons include renewables, lighting, domestic appliances like fridges, home insulation, heating and cooling, energy-efficiency and recycling. In the Store offers advice on seasonal sense, local logic, packaging principles and recycling reason ("In many cases, products made from recycled materials require less energy to produce compared with those made from original materials. For example, it can take almost 75 per cent less energy to make items from recycled steel than it does from new steel.")

It is often hard to find a calculator that offers to work out the footprint of anyone who does not live in North America, Western Europe or somewhere else in an industrialized country. One notable exception is on the Carbon Footprint site. It allows you to work out the emissions from your house, flights, car, motorbike, bus and rail travel, and an intriguing category called Secondary. This covers other possible sources of emissions, including food preferences (vegetarian, organic and so on), fashion, packaging, furniture and electrical appliances, recycling, recreation and use of financial services. And it works not only in the US and Germany but also in such low polluters as Burkina Faso and Tajikistan.

Comparing calculators

If by now you are becoming totally confused about which calculator (if any) will tell you what you want to know, do not despair. The Earth Charter Initiative provides a guide to carbon calculators, a list of countries where they are based, and sites where you may find the one that best suits you. Another site which compares and rates a number of widely-used calculators is the UK-based Climate Outreach and Information Network,

The European Commission's My Carbon Footprint, starts with a challenge: "To find out how much carbon you can save, just mark the changes you would be willing to make in each of our four categories. Our calculator will then work out how many kilos of CO_2 you can save each year and give you the chance to make a public pledge to reduce your personal carbon footprint." The four categories are turning down household appliances, switching them off, recycling, and travel. You do not actually measure your current emissions, but rather estimate the potential savings you would make by applying the measures proposed. The Commission's site comes in all official EU languages and provides links to national carbon calculators in a range of European countries. National calculators are often geared to the specific energy situation of that country and are consequently more accurate than general-purpose calculators that do not ask you to specify your location. Broadly speaking, a GHG calculator is always a trade-off between accuracy and easy applicability for the users: for an accurate calculation you will have to provide a lot of data, while simpler versions apply pre-defined standards to types of house for example or the number of members of a household.

Offset providers and calculators

By the nature of their business, offset providers offer calculators on their websites that determine the climate footprint of your activities and how

Emission Calculators

	Energy				
	Building type	Heating	Lighting	Appliances	Other
World Wide Fund for Nature, UK footprint.wwf.org.uk	X	X	Habits	Habits	Insulation, renewables
Australian Broadcasting Corporation abc.net.au/science/planetslayer/greenhouse_calc.htm	X		Considers the overall energy bill		
Climate Friendly climatefriendly.com/shop					Electricity use
World Resources Institute safeclimate.net/calculator	X	X	Considers the overall energy bill		
Carbon Footprint carbonfootprint.com/calculator.aspx	X	X	Considers the overall energy bill		
atmosfair atmosfair.de [air travel only]					
BP bp.com: Click "Environment" > "Climate Change" > "Carbon footprint calculator" [selected countries]	X	X	Habits	Habits	Insulation, renewables
Myclimate myclimate.org [selected countries]		X			Electricity use
Berkeley Institute of Environment (University of California) bie.berkeley.edu/calculator.swf [US only]	X	X	X	X	
US Environment Protection Agency epa.gov/climatechange/emissions/ind_calculator.html [US only]	X	X	Considers the overall energy bill		
British government actonco2.direct.gov.uk/ [UK only]	X	X	Numbers, habits	Numbers, habits	Insulation, renewables
Australian government [Australia only] environment.gov.au/settlements/gwci/calculator.html	X	X	Considers the overall energy bill		

● Non-profit   ● Profit   ☐ Offset provider

	Transport		Waste	Food	Other	User friendliness
Motor vehicles	Public transportation	Air travel				
Hours spent	Hours spent	Hours spent		Meat, organic, local products		🙂
X	X	X	Recycling yes / no	Meat	Expenses	🙂
X		X				🙂
X		X				🙂
X	X	X	Recycling habits, second hand purchasing	Meat, organic, seasonal products	Recreational, clothes, vehicle choices	🙂
		X				🙂
X	X	X				🙂
X	X	X				🙂
X	X	X		X		🙂
X			CO_2 reduction if recycling			🙂
X	X	X				🙂
X		X	Food and garden waste			🙂

See also: Earth Charter Initiative (earthcharterinaction.org/climate/2007/09/find_the_right_carbon_calculat.html#more);
Climate Outreach and Information Network (coinet.org.uk/materials/carboncalculations); European Commission (www.mycarbonfootprint.eu).

much you need invest to have those emissions reduced somewhere else. So, if you simply want to know what will be the emissions from a specific flight or household operation, they will be quite helpful. The Tufts Climate Institute recommended four companies and their calculators: Myclimate, Climate Friendly, Native Energy and Atmosfair.

The latter is appreciated for estimating emissions from flying which is quite a complex procedure. Factors a good calculator takes into account for flying include the type of ticket (economy passengers generate lower emissions than business or first class ones, because they account for less weight per unit of fuel burnt for each passenger), model of plane (more modern aircraft are more fuel-efficient), occupancy rate (the fewer empty seats there are, the less wasteful empty space is being flown around the world) and the flight distance (a substantial share of the GHG emissions generated from a flight occur during take-off and landing, so longer distance flights are more GHG efficient per unit of distance, and non-stop flights are more GHG efficient than indirect flights). Even if you might not be able to account for this in your calculations, be aware that the total warming effect of your flight is higher than just what is attributed to CO_2 emissions directly. There are other emissions from aviation apart from CO_2, such as nitrogen oxides and water vapour, and CO_2 emitted at high altitude has an enhanced warming effect.

Varying outcomes

Whichever climate calculator you decide to use, you need to remember that there are sometimes huge variations between their conclusions – not surprising when you remember that they often start from quite different assumptions. One calculator, for example, estimated the emissions from a return flight from a European capital to Tokyo at 15.66 tonnes, another at 1.71 tonnes.

Find your own

Before choosing one particular calculator as being best suited to your needs, it is probably worth trying several and comparing their results. Do they explain, in terms you can understand, how they reach their conclusions? What factors does the calculator include, and what does it omit: food, leisure, consumption, transportation? Are the questions the calculator asks you detailed enough to produce useful and honest results, rather than just relying on your rose-tinted view of your own behaviour to give you the answers it thinks you want, not the ones you need?

You may find that two different calculators reach exactly the same conclusions about your carbon footprint, and then give you radically different recommendations for reducing it. They may have perfectly valid reasons for doing so, but it may leave you confused all the same. Ask yourself who has devised them: oil companies and conservation groups both have every right to do so, but it is worth remembering their starting points, and everyone else's.

◎ ORGANIZATIONS

The GHG Protocol Corporate Standard

Inventory frameworks for businesses include the GHG Protocol Corporate Standard and ISO 14064, itself based on the Corporate Standard. Depending on a company's size and financial capacity, it may be worth hiring professional help instead of doing the inventory itself. The Greenhouse Gas Protocol is a widely-used international accounting tool for government and business leaders to understand, quantify and manage greenhouse gas emissions. The protocol is the result of a partnership between the World Resources Institute and the World Business Council for Sustainable Development. The GHG Protocol Corporate Standard provides standards and guidance for companies and other organizations preparing a GHG emissions inventory. It covers the accounting and reporting of all six Kyoto Protocol GHG gases. It was designed with the following objectives in mind:

- to help companies prepare a GHG inventory that represents a true and fair account of their emissions, through the use of standardized approaches and principles;
- simplify and reduce the costs of compiling a GHG inventory;
- provide business with information that can be used to build an effective strategy to manage and reduce GHG emissions;
- increase consistency and transparency in GHG accounting and reporting among various companies and GHG programmes.

The standard builds on the experience and knowledge of over 350 leading experts drawn from businesses, NGOs, governments and accounting associations. It is currently being used by more than 1 000 companies. The GHG Protocol Initiative's vision is to harmonise GHG accounting and reporting standards internationally to ensure that different trading schemes and other climate-related initiatives adopt consistent approaches to GHG accounting.

The GHG Protocol Corporate Standard provides or informs the accounting framework for nearly every organization-level GHG standard and programme in the world, including ISO 14064-1, the EU Emissions Trading Scheme, the California Climate Action Registry, the Climate Registry, the China Energy and GHG Management Programme, and national GHG accounting and reporting programmes in Brazil, Mexico, and the Philippines. It is also the basis for the corporate inventories prepared by over 1000 individual companies, including the Ford Motor Company, Sony, General Electric, Norsk Hydro, DuPont, Shell, BP, IKEA and Nike, and more recently the different organizations of the UN system. www.ghgprotocol.org

More guidance...

Some calculator providers also try to tackle the question of just which emissions you need to calculate. One, the *Carbon Trust*, has come up with a scheme designed to help companies to measure the total amount of carbon emissions produced by their goods and services. This cradle-to-grave analysis, also known as a lifecycle assessment, offers businesses a profile of the pollution caused by their products, from obtaining raw materials through to delivery, consumption and final disposal. Among the services available from the Carbon Trust is a basic carbon footprint indicator which provides an estimated footprint based on a company's energy bill and sector. There is also a carbon footprint calculator which will work out a more sophisticated footprint based on fuel and vehicle usage, electricity bill and employee travel. Life Cycle Analysis is a very recent field of GHG accounting with no internationally accepted standards as yet. Beside Carbon Trust ISO, CDP, and GHGP are all working on this.

For larger enterprises there may need to be some differences in approach to the challenge of calculating GHG emissions. Big corporations have a more complex organizational structure than SMEs and different company groups (e.g. group companies/subsidiaries, associated/affiliated companies, non-incorporated joint ventures/partnerships/operations where partners have joint financial control, franchises, etc.). They may decide on one of two approaches to account for their emissions:

■ the equity share approach – a company accounts for GHG emissions from operations according to its share of equity in the operation. The equity share reflects economic interest, which is the extent of rights a company has to the risks and rewards flowing from an operation;

- the control approach – a company accounts for all the emissions from operations over which it has control, but not for emissions from operations in which it owns an interest but which it does not control. Control can be defined in either financial or operational terms.

Calculating emissions – tools for organizations

The GHG protocol initiative provides a whole range of tools for calculating emissions, some specifically addressing particular sectors or gases, others that are applicable across several sectors. One of these will no doubt provide useful guidance for your particular situation. www.ghgprotocol.org/calculation-tools/all-tools.

The GHG Indicator

UNEP's Energy Branch has produced *The GHG Indicator: UNEP Guidelines for Calculating Greenhouse Gas Emissions for Businesses and Non-Commercial Organizations* to help organizations estimate and report their GHG emissions. The guidelines provide a step-by-step method for converting readily obtained information on fuel and energy use to the GHG emissions that result from them. Emissions arising from different operations and activities – such as manufacturing and transport – are combined to yield a single GHG Indicator, an estimate of the organization's overall contribution to climate change. The method can be used by companies regardless of their size, by government agencies, NGOs and other groups. The guidelines were developed in collaboration with experts from manufacturing companies, accountants, academics, consultants, environmentalists, financial institutions, government agencies and NGOs. Conversion factors used in the guidelines are consistent with those recommended by the IPCC and identical to those adopted by many governments in calculating national GHG emissions: www.uneptie.org/energy/act/ef/GHGin.

The GHG Indicator is useful in several ways. It is a direct response to the Kyoto agreements and thus leads to measures that may be adopted by governments in response to Kyoto, it helps countries or companies with little experience to engage in the GHG accounting process, creating a common reporting platform, and it encourages companies to think and act more environmentally.

━━━ Raw material flow   ━━━ Transformed products flow

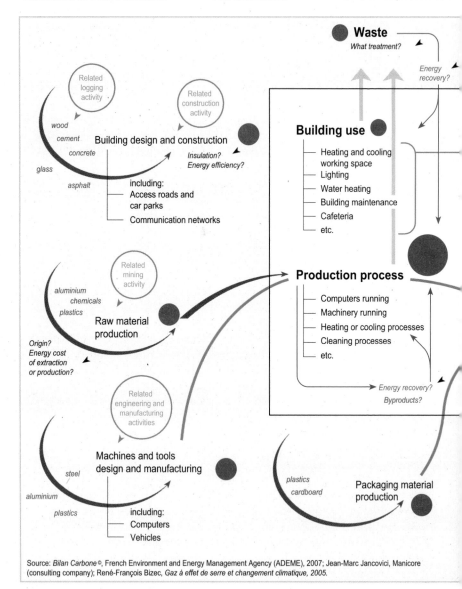

Waste
What treatment?

Energy recovery?

Related logging activity

Related construction activity

wood
cement
concrete
glass
asphalt

Building design and construction

Insulation?
Energy efficiency?

including:
— Access roads and car parks
— Communication networks

Building use
— Heating and cooling working space
— Lighting
— Water heating
— Building maintenance
— Cafeteria
— etc.

Related mining activity

aluminium
chemicals
plastics

Raw material production

Origin?
Energy cost of extraction or production?

Production process
— Computers running
— Machinery running
— Heating or cooling processes
— Cleaning processes
— etc.

Related engineering and manufacturing activities

Energy recovery?
Byproducts?

Machines and tools design and manufacturing

steel
aluminium
plastics

including:
— Computers
— Vehicles

plastics
cardboard

Packaging material production

Source: *Bilan Carbone* ©, French Environment and Energy Management Agency (ADEME), 2007; Jean-Marc Jancovici, Manicore (consulting company); René-François Bizec, *Gaz à effet de serre et changement climatique, 2005.*

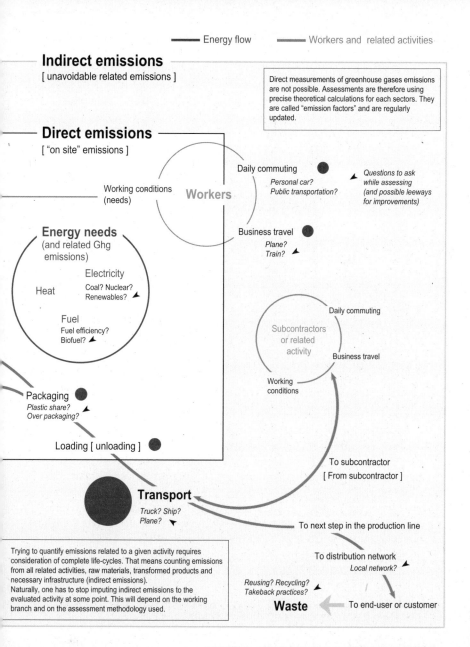

Energy flow ———— **Workers and related activities** ▬▬▬▬

Indirect emissions
[unavoidable related emissions]

Direct measurements of greenhouse gases emissions are not possible. Assessments are therefore using precise theoretical calculations for each sectors. They are called "emission factors" and are regularly updated.

Direct emissions
["on site" emissions]

Working conditions (needs)

Workers

Daily commuting
Personal car?
Public transportation?

Questions to ask while assessing (and possible leeways for improvements)

Business travel
Plane?
Train?

Energy needs
(and related Ghg emissions)

Electricity
Coal? Nuclear?
Renewables? ▲

Heat

Fuel
Fuel efficiency?
Biofuel? ▲

Subcontractors or related activity

Daily commuting

Business travel

Working conditions

Packaging
Plastic share? ▲
Over packaging?

Loading [unloading]

To subcontractor
[From subcontractor]

Transport
Truck? Ship?
Plane? ▼

To next step in the production line

Trying to quantify emissions related to a given activity requires consideration of complete life-cycles. That means counting emissions from all related activities, raw materials, transformed products and necessary infrastructure (indirect emissions).
Naturally, one has to stop imputing indirect emissions to the evaluated activity at some point. This will depend on the working branch and on the assessment methodology used.

To distribution network
Local network? ▲

Reusing? Recycling?
Takeback practices? ▲

Waste

To end-user or customer

CAMSAT – the Carbon Management Self Assessment Tool

Another tool from UNEP's Energy Branch is *CAMSAT – the CArbon Management Self Assessment Tool.* Its purpose is to help organizations assess the quality of their carbon management, and their ability to respond effectively to the challenge: www.uneptie.org/energy/tools/CAMSAT/CAMSAT_index.htm

CAMSAT comprises 23 multiple-choice questions in five sections, covering the major aspects of carbon management (Assessment and Monitoring of GHG Emissions; Emission-reducing Activities; Carbon Offset Strategies; Communication and Reporting; and Assessment of Carbon Risks and Opportunities). The results of the test will provide users with an overall score and identify areas that may require further attention.

Advanced metering

One technology which can help small and medium enterprises to measure their GHG emissions more effectively is ***advanced metering***. The UK's

Advanced metering is designed to provide utility customers with information on a real-time basis about their domestic energy consumption. This information includes data on how much gas and electricity they are consuming, how much it is costing them and what impact their consumption is having on greenhouse gas emissions. Advanced metering is a process for achieving significant energy and cost savings. Efforts are under way to make advanced metering technology available for SMEs as well. As considerable investment is involved, cost savings so far are possible only on annual energy bills of €60 000 (US$96 000) or more.

Carbon Trust says its use by SMEs could save 2.5 million tonnes of CO_2 emissions per year – equivalent to the entire annual carbon footprint of a medium-sized city. Over three years the Trust installed advanced meters at more than 580 sites across the UK and found that by switching to them SMEs could on average identify potential carbon savings of over 12 per cent and successfully achieve savings of more than 5 per cent. On average, the companies in the trial saved over £1 000 (US$2 000) a year on energy. The greatest savings went to multi-site businesses, such as retail and wholesale chains, and to high energy users like small manufacturing companies. Widespread adoption of advanced metering by British SMEs would result in annual cost savings of £300 million (US$600 million) for small businesses, the Trust concludes.

Calculators

The *Carbon Neutral Company* (www.carbonneutral.com) has a calculator designed for use by business but does not assume it will necessarily suit everybody. So it provides bespoke calculators designed for individual companies who think they need more sophisticated help.

There is a greenhouse gas event calculator devised by Climate Neutral (www.climatecalculator.org). It is limited to the US, offers CO_2 emissions calculations, and is concerned with the amount of carbon your guests will generate by travelling to an event you are holding.

BT *British Telecom* is one of the world's leading providers of communications solutions and services, servicing around 18 million customers in 170 countries in Europe, the Americas and Asia-Pacific. BT employs over 106 000 people worldwide. It set its first carbon reduction target in 1992 and has already reduced its own UK CO_2 emissions by 60 per cent on 1996 levels. In 2007, BT developed a new strategy to further reduce its CO_2 emissions to 80 per cent below 1996 levels. The climate change strategy has four elements, and sets out how BT will reduce its footprint; influence its customers; influence its suppliers; and engage its employees. Using one of the UK's largest computer-based monitoring and targeting systems, it collects data at half-hour intervals from more than 6 000 sites. This has helped the company identify wasted energy earlier than by relying on a monthly bill. BT reports its emissions according to the inventory guidelines in the Greenhouse Gas Protocol.

CITIES

Up to now cities that wanted to calculate their GHG emissions either followed their own path or adopted an inventory tool designed for business. ICLEI-Local Governments for Sustainability has now released a draft International Local Government Greenhouse Gas Protocol with two parts: the Emissions Analysis Protocol provides guidance on making an inventory of greenhouse gas emissions and reporting them, and the Measures Analysis Protocol provides guidance on quantifying the emission reduction benefits of mitigation policies and projects. The Protocol goes hand-in-hand with an on-line software tool to plan, monitor and report on GHG emissions and to be released towards the end of 2008 for use by local governments around the globe. www.iclei.org/ghgprotocol.

The UN Framework Convention on Climate Change spells out in detail the way in which countries are to monitor and report their GHG emissions. Doing this accurately and comprehensively as well as covering all countries is obviously central to developing policies for tackling climate change.

Under the Kyoto Protocol national governments are asked to calculate their GHG emissions, and the Annex 1 ("developed") countries' reports have been audited by the UNFCCC at least twice.

Verifying and reporting your emissions

Once the inventory is complete according to the definition you have chosen, it might by of interest to have it independently verified by a third-party certifier. Verification determines whether an inventory is free of material misstatement. The need for verification depends very much on the intended purpose of the inventory. If it is intended to comply with regulations, or to be widely disseminated to the public, for example, then strict quality control measures are necessary and verification may well play a role. Verification is expensive and the efforts should be worth it, as for example with emission trading: in order to trade GHG allowances with other systems, data must be transparent and verifiable.

The need for verification is also determined by the GHG programme you chose to report to. There are numerous voluntary or mandatory international, national, sub-national, government or non-governmental authorities that register, certify, or regulate GHG emissions or removals independently of the company.

Analyse:
How are we doing? And what about everyone else?

When you publish the inventory you make it accessible to anyone who may be interested (depending, of course, on the nature and size of your organization – as an individual, you might want to talk to your neighbours, friends, family, as a company to your shareholders, as a public administration to your citizens etc.). This can help to show up any gaps or problems – or any opportunities for those trying to emulate you – and it will make your efforts more credible.

You now also need to analyse the risks and opportunities related to GHG emissions, by looking at what others have learned and done. This will include information on benchmarking and determining sources of risk and opportunity. Evaluating what other people have done, perhaps at other levels, provides additional insights and allows us to see where we stand in regard to others.

The Climate Disclosure Standards Board (CDSB) is a consortium of seven business and environmental organizations formed to jointly advocate a generally accepted framework for corporations to report climate change risks and opportunities, carbon footprints, and carbon reduction strategies and their implications for shareholder value. By aligning their basic requests for information, CDSB members aim to go beyond best practice and to make it standard practice for companies to report climate change-related information in their Annual Reports and for this to extend into related analysis by the investment research community. CDSB was convened at the 2007 annual meeting of the World Economic Forum in response to increasing calls for action from corporations and financial markets to address global warming and the associated growth of climate change information collection and reporting initiatives.

Analyse what the Kyoto Protocol has or has not achieved in reducing the GHG emissions of industrialized countries, and in trying to persuade other nations to join emissions reduction efforts. See what success various countries have had with legislation designed to reduce urban traffic congestion, or to curb fuel consumption, or to decarbonise their economies. Learn from others' triumphs and disasters. And make sure they are able to learn from yours: the more proficient you are at reducing your GHG emissions, the more competitive advantage you can claim.

The UN Environment Programme has launched the Climate Neutral Network (CN Net), an initiative designed to help companies, cities and countries make radical cuts in greenhouse gas emissions and exchange their experiences in this process.

Greenhouse gas programmes	Type
California Climate Action Registry www.climateregistry.org	Voluntary registry
US Environmental Protection Agency **Climate Leaders** www.epa.gov/climateleaders	Voluntary reduction programme
World Wide Fund for Nature **Climate Savers** www.worldwildlife.org/climatesavers	Voluntary registry
World Economic Forum **Global Greenhouse Gas Register** www.weforum.org	Voluntary registry
European Union **Greenhouse Gas Emission** **Allowance Trading Scheme** ec.europa.eu/environment/climat/emission.htm	Mandatory allowance trading scheme
European Pollutant Emission Register www.eper.ec.europa.eu/eper	Mandatory register for large industrial facilities
Chicago Climate Exchange www.chicagoclimateexchange.com	Voluntary allowance trading scheme
Respect Europe **Business Leaders Initiative on Climate Change** www.respecteurope.com	Voluntary reduction programme

Focus	Gases covered	Boundaries
Organizations	CO_2 for the first 3 years, six Kyoto gases thereafter	Equity share or control for California or US operations
Organizations	Six Kyoto gases (CO_2, CH_4, N_2O, PFCs, HFCs, SF_6)	Equity share or control for US operations at a minimum
Organizations	CO_2	Equity share or control for worldwide operations
Organizations	Six Kyoto gases	Equity share or control for worldwide operations
Facilities	Six Kyoto gases	Facilities in selected sectors
Facilities	Six Kyoto gases and other pollutants	Facilities falling under EU IPPC directive
Organizations and projects	Six Kyoto gases	Equity share
Organizations	Six Kyoto gases	Equity share or control for worldwide operations

Source: Greenhouse Gas Protocol Initiative, *Greenhouse Gas Protocol Corporate Standard*, page 90.

Climate Change Performance Index 2008

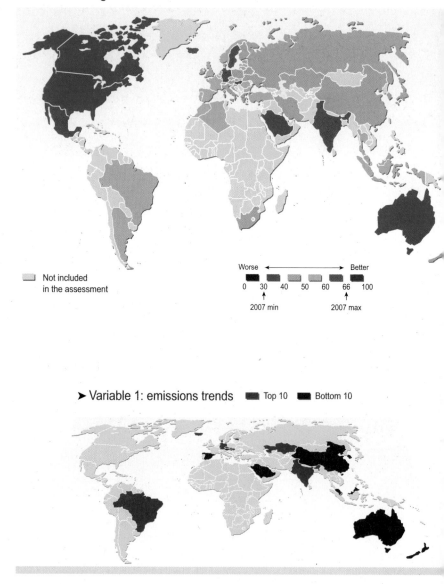

Not included in the assessment

Worse ← → Better

0 30 40 50 60 66 100

2007 min   2007 max

➤ Variable 1: emissions trends   ■ Top 10   ■ Bottom 10

The Climate Change Performance Index developed by Germanwatch is calculated using three weighted indexes:

➤ Emissions trends for energy, transport, industry and residential account for 50% of total rating;
➤ A country's current emissions level (CO_2 emitted per primary energy unit, primary energy unit per GDP, primary energy unit per capita) is given a 30% weight in the overall evaluation;
➤ Climate policy (national and international) weighs 20%.

Source: Germanwatch, *The Climate Change Performance Index, A Comparison of Emissions Trends and Climate Protection Policies of the Top 56 CO_2 Emitting Nations*, December 2007.

➤ Variable 2: emissions level   ■ Top 10   ■ Bottom 10

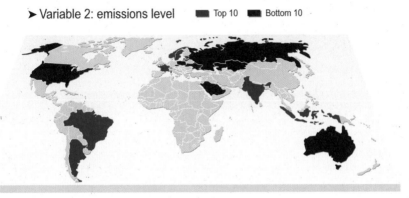

➤ Variable 3: climate policy   ■ Top 10   ■ Bottom 10

The climate costs of the United Nations

To address the growing challenge of climate change and the urgency to take concrete action at all levels, the UN Secretary-General has urged UN agencies to respond collectively and lead by example in greening the UN and becoming climate neutral. He has tasked a body called the UN Environmental Management Group (EMG) to coordinate a collective UN system-wide effort to move the UN's operations towards climate neutrality.

In October 2007 with the support of the EMG, the UN Secretary-General and the Heads of UN agencies agreed on a strategy to move their respective organizations towards climate neutrality. They made a commitment to estimate their GHG emissions in conformity with international standards

THE CLIMATE NEUTRAL NETWORK

Launched in February 2008, the CN Net began with four national governments – Costa Rica, Iceland, Norway and New Zealand – and several cities and corporations, all committed to working towards climate neutrality, as founder members. CN Net is an information exchange platform not only for existing members but for all nations, local governments and businesses which seek to cut their net GHG emissions to zero.

The founder states acknowledge that there are real problems on the road to climate-neutral economies. Norway's main challenge, for example, is limiting fossil fuel emissions. The world's third largest exporter of oil aims to become climate-neutral by 2030, with global carbon offsets accounting for part of the target, and carbon sequestration (see page 88) – a method of trapping emitted gases and storing them underground or beneath the sea – helping to reduce its domestic emissions. Norway also plans to expand public transport and reduce taxes for new, fuel-efficient cars.

In New Zealand agriculture accounts for half of all greenhouse gases, with the country's tens of millions of farm animals producing large quantities of methane. The country plans to raise its already high use of renewable resources for electricity generation (predominantly hydropower at present) to 90 per cent by the end of 2009, undertake efforts to reduce greenhouse gas emissions as far as possible, and to analyse the cost implications and explore the budgetary modalities of purchasing carbon offsets to ultimately achieve climate neutrality.

Over the coming months and years, the EMG will be supporting these efforts in close cooperation with the UNEP's Paris-based Division of Technology, Industry and Economics, which leads a facility called the Sustainable United Nations (SUN). Together they will provide assistance to the UN agencies to calculate their GHG emissions according to the highest environmental standards, develop individual agency's plans for reducing their footprint, adopt a common approach for purchasing offsets, and also advance other aspects related to greening the UN, such sustainable procurement.

by 2025 and to halve per capita transport emissions by 2040 by using electric cars and biofuels. Iceland aims to reduce its net greenhouse gas emissions – which come mainly from transport and industry – by 75 per cent before 2050. Carbon sequestration in vegetation is an important factor in Iceland's climate strategy. It has suffered the worst soil erosion of any European country since its settlement 1 100 years ago, with deforestation leaving the fragile volcanic soil at the mercy of wind and water erosion. Costa Rica is aiming for climate neutrality by 2021, to be achieved by taxes and incentives to protect forests and encourage carbon storage and sequestration.

The four cities signed up to CN Net are Arendal in Norway, Vancouver on the west coast of Canada, Växjö in southern Sweden and Rizhao in northern China. Ninety-nine per cent of urban households in Rizhao, Shandong province, have solar water heaters. The amount of energy used for each unit of economic output has fallen by almost a third on 2000 levels and CO_2 emissions by almost half.

The latest wave of participants extends the initiative's reach to small and medium enterprises, as well as international, non-governmental and research organizations. www.climateneutral.unep.org.

Act

There is, ultimately, no substitute for action – once you have thought about what you want to do and how you are going to do it. And taking action to work towards climate neutrality can unlock potential you may not realise you possess. Mention climate change to a lot of people, and the instant response is often a sort of paralysis. If they know what they need to do they probably have little idea how to do it, or whether they can even make a start. So one clear message to give them is that there is something they can do, that it is both worth doing and do-able, and that they can do it without waiting for anyone else.

Nor need you look very far to find a starting point. Carbon alone is embedded in almost everything we use, or do, and the other main greenhouse gases are involved in the production and consumption of many parts of life that we take for granted (see the first chapter of this guide for a reminder). So you can probably make progress towards a more climate-neutral way of life every minute.

But, at the risk of stating the obvious, some things are more worthwhile than others, and some steps you decide to take will make more sense at one point than at others. To be specific, there is a logical way of acting that will yield the largest dividends most quickly, a sequence that is worth trying to follow:

➜ For the most effective results, the biggest bang for your buck, you will need to focus at first on whatever makes up the biggest chunk of your emissions. Over time the proportions will change, and other sources may become more important.

➜ Wherever you can, avoid using or consuming anything that will increase the GHG emissions for which you accept responsibility.

➜ Where possible choose the option that will let you actually reduce them, for example by increasing the efficiency of your activities.

➜ Do not let yourself be locked into a familiar way of doing things when something better comes along. Keep an open mind regarding the potential of new technologies.

➜ After you have reduced as much as you can, offset your emissions. Off-setting is sometimes seen as **a charged and contentious issue,** but it may

Some say that offsetting lets you off the hook, discourages action of those who can afford to pay for their climate sins but who also happen to be in many cases those with the biggest climate impact. Consequently, the energy intensive structures remain, climate conscious innovations receive less support and behaviour patterns do not change. On the other side, climate neutrality is hardly possible without the option of offsetting. And the atmosphere eventually does not care where the GHG emissions come from. So considering that for activities such as flying or cement production no large scale low-emission solution is in sight for the near future, it may be a good idea to utilize the money those businesses generate for helping such cases where efficient technology exists, but is not affordable to those who are responsible. It also allows also to disseminate climate neutral possibilities to those who may not have resources. Under the premise "First reduce what you can, then offset the remainder", the different aspects are combined in order to yield the most benefits for all parties concerned, i.e. everyone.

be a valid option.

Think too about what it will be easiest to do, not that you will be able to do everything easily – you will not – but because it may make sense to start with the simpler steps before launching yourself onto something more ambitious. It is relatively easy, for example, to take action that will affect you alone, and less easy if what you do is going to have an impact on your employees, or shareholders, or voters. It is easier to act when there is some sort of support you can call on: if your government encourages people to produce renewable energy by paying them for the surplus they can supply to the national grid, you may well be tempted down that route yourself. But if there is little practical support for renewables you may well feel it is a step too far for you until things change.

Start with free options and work up to more expensive options later. If you think you should replace your city's public transport system with less-polluting vehicles but cannot see how to afford it, then go for something you can afford that will take you in the same direction: encouraging cycling, perhaps, by making it safer on the city streets, or integrating the various urban transport systems so that one ticket will be valid on bus, tram, train and metro (and if that seems blindingly obvious, it is still a daring innovation to city planners in some industrialized countries).

Consumer 🔍

★ ★ Buy high-quality, long lasting products
★ Consult reputable eco-standards or consumers' associations before buying
Choose local products
★ Choose seasonal products
★ Try organic products
★ Drink tap water
★ Reduce meat consumption
Avoid shrimps
Choose products with limited packaging

Follow the "3Rs":
Reduce
Reuse
Recycle

Resident ●

Daily deeds
Take showers instead of baths ★
Turn off electric devices when not using them ★
(make sure they don't remain in stand-by mode)
Turn off the light when leaving a room ★
Sort your garbage
Collect rain water for the garden ★
Choose low energy bulbs ★ ★
Put a lid on pans when boiling water ★
Run washing machines during slack hours

Energy efficiency at home
Improve insulation (windows, roof, walls) ★ ★
Replace very old electric devices ★ ★
Use water-saving tap inserts ★
Use water-saving shower heads ★

Planning to become an owner?
Choose collective instead of individual building ★
Choose ecological material, locally extracted and manufactured ★ ★
Choose renewable energies ★ ★

On the move 🔗

Leisure traveler
Travel less and closer ★
Limit flying
Limit car use

Driver ◄——
Replace very old cars ★ ★
Avoid SUVs ★
Limit your speed ★
Drive with fluidity ★
Respect pedestrians and bikers

Commuter
Use your car only if no other option
and in that case organize carpools ★
Bike or walk ★
Use public transport ★

Business traveler
Make sure your travel is necessary
Use video conferencing ★ ★
Choose a neutral way to travel when possible
Use public transportation ★

Source: UNEP / GRID-Arendal, 2008.

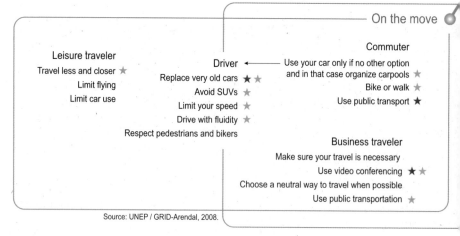

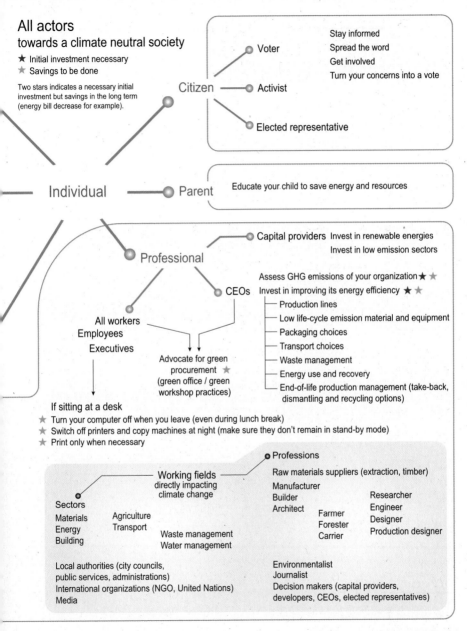

All actors
towards a climate neutral society

★ Initial investment necessary
★ Savings to be done

Two stars indicates a necessary initial investment but savings in the long term (energy bill decrease for example).

Individual

Citizen

- Voter
- Activist
- Elected representative

Stay informed
Spread the word
Get involved
Turn your concerns into a vote

Parent   Educate your child to save energy and resources

Professional

Capital providers   Invest in renewable energies
Invest in low emission sectors

CEOs

Assess GHG emissions of your organization ★ ★
Invest in improving its energy efficiency ★ ★
— Production lines
— Low life-cycle emission material and equipment
— Packaging choices
— Transport choices
— Waste management
— Energy use and recovery
— End-of-life production management (take-back, dismantling and recycling options)

All workers
Employees
Executives

Advocate for green procurement ★
(green office / green workshop practices)

If sitting at a desk
★ Turn your computer off when you leave (even during lunch break)
★ Switch off printers and copy machines at night (make sure they don't remain in stand-by mode)
★ Print only when necessary

Working fields
directly impacting
climate change

Professions
Raw materials suppliers (extraction, timber)
Manufacturer
Builder   Researcher
Architect   Engineer
              Farmer   Designer
              Forester   Production designer
              Carrier

Sectors
Materials   Agriculture
Energy   Transport
Building   Waste management
                  Water management

Local authorities (city councils, public services, administrations)
International organizations (NGO, United Nations)
Media

Environmentalist
Journalist
Decision makers (capital providers, developers, CEOs, elected representatives)

High-emitting facilities

Cement factories

Power plants

Gas processing plants   Refineries

Iron and steel manufacturing

Chemical industries (ammonia, hydrogen, ethylene, ethanol, etc.)

Set clear priorities in **Research and Development** allocation of funds

— Set performance standards ★

— Control them ★

— Switch to cleaner technologies

>> | see all boxed pieces of text |

| Carbon Capture and Storage |

— Nuclear ★ ★   ◄ *Nuclear waste management highly problematic, remaining risks of nuclear accidents*

— Subsidize possibilities of | industrial reconversion | for sectors inherently emitting too much ★

Transport

— Expand the national public transport network

— Freight

— Increase taxes for trucking freight

— Develop rail and river freight alternatives ★

— Advocate speed limits for international bunker freight shipping ★

— Technological improvements

— Vehicle design

| Hull shape and propellers of ships |
| Plane engines and wings |
| Engines and exhaust systems of cars |

— Type of fuel   *Land use competition with food production, intensive agriculture*

— Biofuels ★

— From heavy fuel oil to marine diesel oil for ships

— Operational measures for ships and planes ★

— Better routing and timing for ships

— Better air traffic management (no waiting for landing)

— Apply fossil fuel taxes to air traffic and shipping

— Stop fossil fuel subsidies   *Equity problem (weighs more heavily on poor population)*

— Increase taxes on vehicle purchase and registration, and on use of roads and car parks ★

Energy

— Subisidize | renewable energy | projects, in all fields

Solar   Ocean
Wind
Geothermal   Biomass
Hydro-energy

— Subsidize | energy efficiency | improvement projects

Awareness-raising / educational campaigns

Agriculture and forestry

— Limit / control the use of fertilizers and pesticides

— Stop subsidies to intensive farming ★

— Preserve biological sinks such as forests (stop deforestation) ★

— Promote sustainable logging (labelling)

— Control peat fires

— Subsidize greener farming practices and organic agriculture

— Produce for the local market ("food sovereignty" vs. global market)

GHG assessments of public sector and local authorities

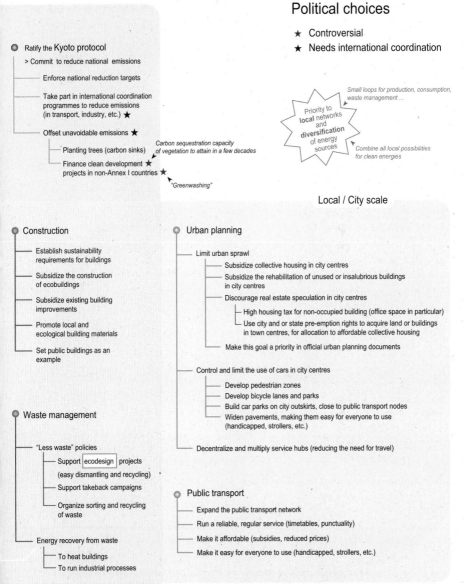

Political choices

★ Controversial
★ Needs international coordination

Ratify the **Kyoto protocol**
> Commit to reduce national emissions

Enforce national reduction targets

Take part in international coordination programmes to reduce emissions (in transport, industry, etc.) ★

Offset unavoidable emissions ★

Planting trees (carbon sinks) — *Carbon sequestration capacity of vegetation to attain in a few decades*

Finance clean development ★ projects in non-Annex I countries ★

"Greenwashing"

Priority to local networks and diversification of energy sources

Small loops for production, consumption, waste management ...

Combine all local possibilities for clean energies

Local / City scale

Construction

Establish sustainability requirements for buildings

Subsidize the construction of ecobuildings

Subsidize existing building improvements

Promote local and ecological building materials

Set public buildings as an example

Waste management

"Less waste" policies

Support ecodesign projects (easy dismantling and recycling)

Support takeback campaigns

Organize sorting and recycling of waste

Energy recovery from waste

To heat buildings

To run industrial processes

Urban planning

Limit urban sprawl

Subsidize collective housing in city centres

Subsidize the rehabilitation of unused or insalubrious buildings in city centres

Discourage real estate speculation in city centres

High housing tax for non-occupied building (office space in particular)

Use city and or state pre-emption rights to acquire land or buildings in town centres, for allocation to affordable collective housing

Make this goal a priority in official urban planning documents

Control and limit the use of cars in city centres

Develop pedestrian zones

Develop bicycle lanes and parks

Build car parks on city outskirts, close to public transport nodes

Widen pavements, making them easy for everyone to use (handicapped, strollers, etc.)

Decentralize and multiply service hubs (reducing the need for travel)

Public transport

Expand the public transport network

Run a reliable, regular service (timetables, punctuality)

Make it affordable (subsidies, reduced prices)

Make it easy for everyone to use (handicapped, strollers, etc.)

Source: *Mitigation of Climate Change*, Working Group III, Fourth Assessment Report of the Intergovernmental Panel on Climate Change, 2007.

Think about whether you should start by acting directly to reduce or, if possible, eliminate GHG emissions, or whether you might do better to use indirect means. If you are in government, perhaps, you can take direct action by increasing taxation on motorists who drive large "gas-guzzlers". But equally, and perhaps more constructively, you could leave them well alone, and instead reduce taxation on those who try to be frugal with their emissions.

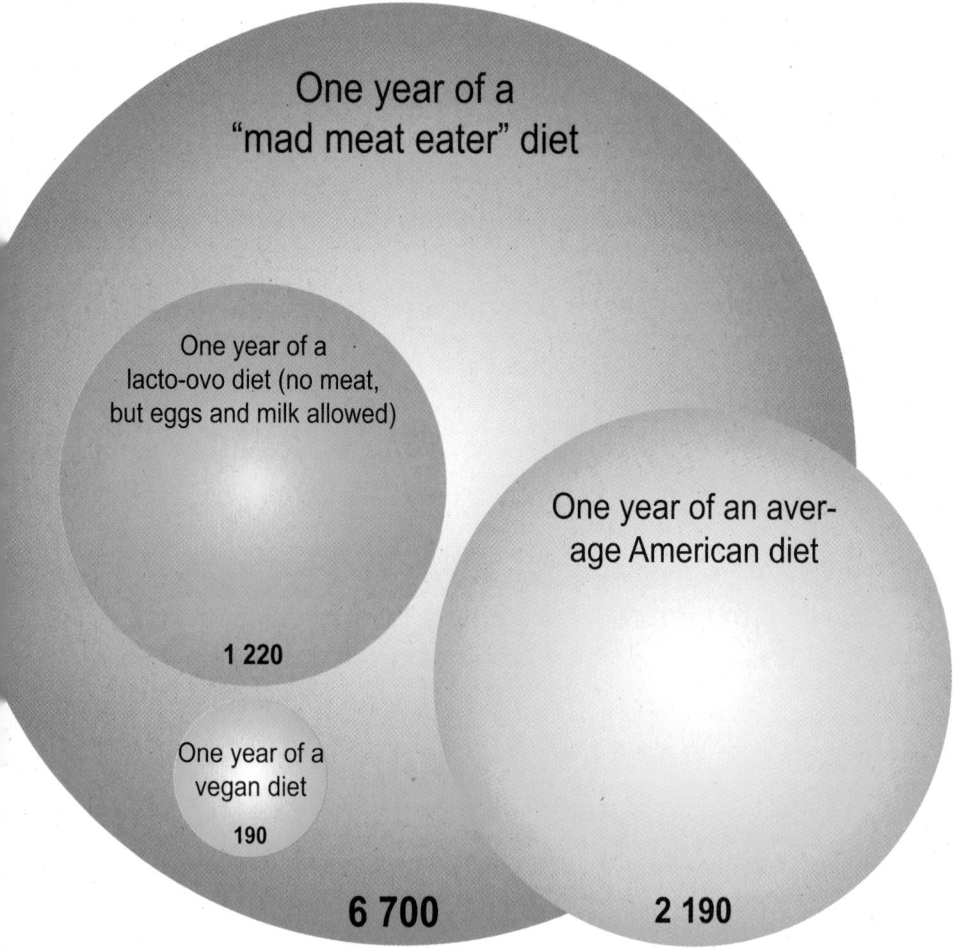

One year of a
"mad meat eater" diet

One year of a
lacto-ovo diet (no meat,
but eggs and milk allowed)

One year of an average American diet

1 220

One year of a
vegan diet
190

6 700

2 190

In this way there are many things each of us, and many of the groups we belong to, can do to have an indirect impact on reducing emissions. For example, consumers will push producers by the choices they make, and businesses can require their suppliers to provide them with climate-friendly products and services. At the same time cities can provide the infrastructure to get around town to find products in the most climate efficient way. Many potential decisions stem from political choices – individuals will follow market forces (e.g. decisions on home insulation, for instance, will be based on affordability, incentives and disincentives); business leaders are increasingly keen to have a political framework in which to operate.

It is crucial to be aware of how we influence others. We should remember that when we act and make sure our own record is exemplary before trying to teach others lessons. Particularly if we want any credibility.

Furthermore, what might seem insignificant in a global perspective may well considerably reduce your personal climate impact. In other words, your small contribution may only be a drop in the ocean, but all of our efforts taken together will definitely help to alleviate the GHG burden on the atmosphere.

The Credit Suisse bank aims to achieve climate neutrality by 2009. Three-quarters of its CO_2 emissions come from the energy used to run its offices, so it has made a gradual switch to renewable power supplies, and is replacing oil and gas heating with heat pumps or district heating. In 2007 it was able to disconnect more than 2 000 of its servers, 10 per cent of the total. The waste heat generated by the computers used by Credit Suisse staff at its Zurich office is diverted to heat nearby offices and homes. Its Hong Kong offices use network PCs without hard disk servers, which can cut electricity consumption by 20 per cent. In 2006 the bank's use of video conferencing was 30 per cent up on the previous year; it encourages staff to use trains rather than planes for short journeys, and has begun working towards using carbon-neutral flight tickets. By 2006 the bank's Swiss operations were GHG-neutral, with some of the saving achieved by buying carbon offsets.

Running a European freezer for a year **18** **48** Running a US freezer for a year

CARBON SINKS AND SEQUESTRATION

The opposite of a GHG source is a GHG sink. A sink is any process, activity or mechanism that removes a greenhouse gas, an aerosol or a precursor of a greenhouse gas or aerosol from the atmosphere.

Natural sinks for CO_2 are for example forests, soils and oceans. It is also possible to enhance naturally occurring processes or use modern technology to remove CO_2 from the atmosphere and store it in reservoirs. The uptake of CO_2 in a reservoir, whether natural or artificial is also called carbon sequestration.

Biological sequestration in forests

The role of forests in carbon sequestration is probably best understood and appears to offer the greatest near-term potential for human management. Unlike many plants and most crops, which have short lives or release much of their carbon at the end of each season, forest biomass accumulates carbon over decades and centuries. Furthermore, forests can accumulate large amounts of CO_2 in relatively short periods, typically several decades. *Afforestation and reforestation* are measures that can be taken to

Afforestation refers to establishing forest by natural succession or planting trees on land where they did not formerly grow. Reforestation means re-establishing forest, either by natural regeneration or by planting in an area where forest was removed.

enhance biological carbon sequestration. The IPCC calculated that a global programme to 2050 involving reduced deforestation, enhanced natural regeneration of tropical forests and worldwide re-afforestation could sequester 60–87 thousand million tonnes of atmospheric carbon, equivalent to some 12–15 per cent of projected CO_2 emissions from fossil fuel burning for that period.

As one of the countries in the CN Net, Costa Rica is focusing on its considerable potential for using forests to become climate neutral.

Geological sequestration beneath the Earth's surface

The second option, carbon capture and storage (CCS) has been discussed for decades as a possible way of solving the climate crisis. As it stands, it

Carbon **sequestered** annually by 100 sq m of forest preserved from deforestation

3 500

involves capturing CO_2 emissions and storing them in geological formations that originally contained fossil fuels. CO_2 emissions, for example from fossil fuel combustion, are captured and deposited beneath the Earth's surface in depleted oil and gas wells, deep coal seams or aquifers (subterranean zones of water-bearing rock or sand). There are three basic technologies: absorption (take-up of a gas into the interior of a solid or liquid), adsorption (the gas is taken up in the form of a layer on the surface of a solid), and gas separation membranes.

Ocean sequestration beneath the surface

The ocean can hold enormous quantities of CO_2 because unlike most atmospheric gases it reacts with water to form carbonate and bicarbonate greatly enhancing its solubility. It is estimated to hold about 38 000 Gigatonnes of dissolved inorganic carbon (DIC). In comparison, the world's total fossil carbon reserves, including conventional and unconventional deposits of oil, natural gas and coal, are estimated at about 6 500 Gigatonnes of Carbon (GtC), so if all of them were burned and the CO_2 sequestrated in the deep ocean, the DIC content would only increase about 17 per cent to 44 500 GtC.

Carbon stored by forests

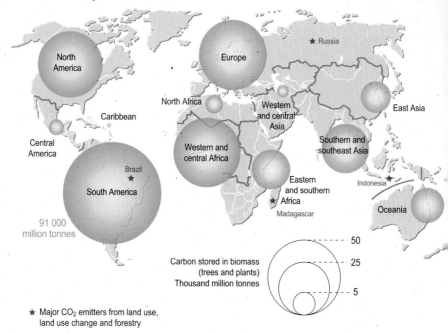

North America

Europe

★ Russia

North Africa

Western and central Asia

East Asia

Caribbean

Central America

Western and central Africa

Southern and southeast Asia

Brazil ★

South America

Eastern and southern Africa

★

Indonesia ★

Madagascar

Oceania

91 000 million tonnes

Carbon stored in biomass (trees and plants) Thousand million tonnes

------ 50

-- 25

-- 5

★ Major CO_2 emitters from land use, land use change and forestry

Distribution of carbon inventory

As a percentage of average carbon inventory

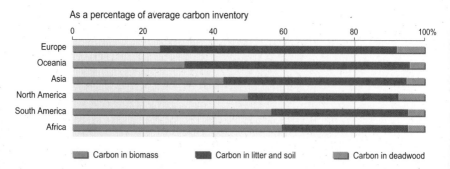

	0	20	40	60	80	100%
Europe						
Oceania						
Asia						
North America						
South America						
Africa						

■ Carbon in biomass   ■ Carbon in litter and soil   ■ Carbon in deadwood

Carbon inventory

"*Forests play a vital role in the global carbon cycle, storing roughly half of the world's terrestrial carbon (Millennium Ecosystem Asessment, 2005). When forests grow, they withdraw carbon dioxide from the atmosphere and sequester it in trees and soil. When they are destroyed or degraded, much of this carbon is released, either immediately if the trees are burned or more slowly if the organic matter decays naturally.*"
EarthTrends Update, April 2008.

Sources: *Atlas Environnement du Monde Diplomatique*, 2007; *Global Forest Resources Assessment 2005*, United Nations Food and Agriculture Organization (FAO); Hadley climate research unit, 2007; World Resources Institute (WRI), *EarthTrends Environmental Information Portal*, 2008; World Resources Institute, *Climate Analysis Indicators Tool*, 2008.

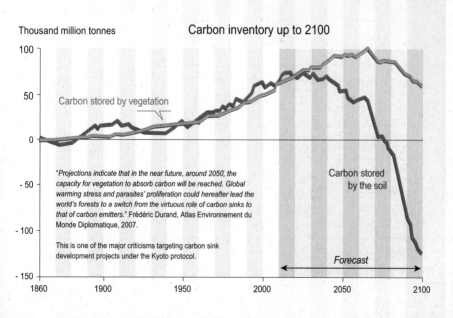

Carbon inventory up to 2100

Thousand million tonnes

Carbon stored by vegetation

"*Projections indicate that in the near future, around 2050, the capacity for vegetation to absorb carbon will be reached. Global warming stress and parasites' proliferation could hereafter lead the world's forests to a switch from the virtuous role of carbon sinks to that of carbon emitters.*" Frédéric Durand, Atlas Environnement du Monde Diplomatique, 2007.

This is one of the major criticisms targeting carbon sink development projects under the Kyoto protocol.

Carbon stored by the soil

Forecast

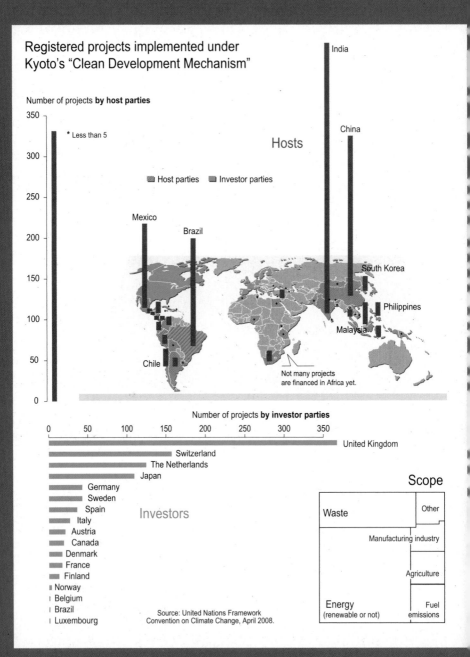

Registered projects implemented under Kyoto's "Clean Development Mechanism"

Number of projects **by host parties**

* Less than 5

Hosts

Host parties   Investor parties

India

China

Mexico

Brazil

South Korea

Philippines

Malaysia

Chile

Not many projects are financed in Africa yet.

350
300
250
200
150
100
50
0

Number of projects **by investor parties**

0   50   100   150   200   250   300   350

United Kingdom
Switzerland
The Netherlands
Japan
Germany
Sweden
Spain
Italy
Austria
Canada
Denmark
France
Finland
Norway
Belgium
Brazil
Luxembourg

Investors

Scope

Waste   Other

                    Manufacturing industry

                              Agriculture

Energy   Fuel
(renewable or not)   emissions

Source: United Nations Framework
Convention on Climate Change, April 2008.

There are two main ways of storing CO_2 in the oceans: by capturing it and injecting it into the ocean at depths of 1 000–1 500 metres, and by enhancing natural ocean uptake of CO_2. There are natural processes that, together, gradually remove CO_2 from the surface of the oceans and deposit it at greater depths.

The IPCC has estimated that some 40 GtC could be stored in depleted oil wells, some 90 GtC in depleted gas wells and some 20 GtC via enhanced oil recovery. Global carbon emissions in 2000 where 6 GtC which means that, at present levels, about 25 years' worth of global emissions could be stored in this way. However, capturing and compressing CO_2 requires a great deal of energy and would increase the fuel consumption of a plant equipped with CCS. The cost of CCS depends on the cost of capture and storage which in varies according to the method used. The IPCC estimates that the cost of storing one tonne of CO_2 in a geological formation ranges from US$0.5 to 8, plus an additional US$0.10 to 0.30 for monitoring costs. Ocean storage cost estimates vary between US$6 and 30.

A Norwegian company, Statoil, has been successfully sequestering about 1 million tonnes of CO_2 a year since 1996. It is using the Utsira formation, a saline aquifer located 800 metres below the sea bed, beneath its Sleipner West gas production platform in the North Sea.

Statoil has calculated that the Utsira formation could store some 1 000 million tonnes of CO_2 a year – roughly equivalent to the current total of CO_2 emissions from all of the EU's electric power plants for the next 600 years.

Act: **Reduce**

Reducing the GHG emissions for which you are responsible should be satisfying but will probably sometimes seem a thankless task. But never forget that other people will be watching you, and that you wield a lot of influence. One of the most significant gains from reducing your own climate footprint is the example you set. A couple of instances are the abandoning of CFC spray cans after the Montreal Protocol, which sharply reduced ozone-damaging gases, and the banning of polystyrene foam containers by well-known fast-food restaurants.

One of the strongest arguments for reducing GHG emissions is that it will often save money. Energy prices across the world are rising, making it harder to afford to travel, heat and light homes and factories, and keep a modern economy ticking over. So it is both common sense and climate sense to use energy as sparingly as possible.

When the example comes from people or groups who already enjoy high public standing, the results can be even more far-reaching. For many people today, some of the most influential people are footballers. So when the British club Ipswich Town chose to do something about climate change by becoming carbon-neutral, a lot of people were watching. The club worked out that it produced 3 200 tonnes of CO_2 every season and successfully offset this by asking supporters to make specific pledges to save energy. The incentive was football-based: when the club hit its target of 14 000 pledges, it was rewarded with a significant sum of money towards transfers by its main sponsor. The fans were encouraged to reach the target by committing themselves to take simple steps like using public transport and high-efficiency light bulbs and turning down their boilers, while some of the players turned to car-pooling. Another club, Manchester City, has begun producing its own energy, building a wind turbine to provide all the electricity for its stadium, and selling the additional 20 per cent surplus.

You do not need to be a football club to encourage others. As an individual you will reach your friends and neighbours, as a small company your clients, as a multinational your suppliers and customers, as a city of course your inhabitants but also other towns and the same is valid for countries (see CN Net).

What we use and produce

Beyond the emissions we cause directly for example by driving a car or heating our home, there are other obvious ways to slim down our production of greenhouse gases, in particular by reducing the climate impact of the goods we produce and use.

The virtuous cycle of steadily reducing emissions will result from a more critical **approach to consumption.** That in turn will benefit from better and

> When calculating the climate impact of the goods and services we consume, it is crucial to look at every step in the product's life. A system, or life cycle, can begin when extracting raw materials from the ground and generating energy. Materials and energy are then part of manufacturing, transportation, use (wearing and washing the T-shirt, for instance), and eventually recycling, reuse, or disposal. A life cycle approach demonstrates how our purchase and use of a product are only part of a whole train of events. Having the whole life cycle of a product in mind helps us make conscious choices when buying electricity, meat or a new T-shirt. Then we may recognize that we do have an influence on what happens at each of these stages, letting us balance trade-offs and positively affect the economy, the environment, and society.
>
> There are well established Life Cycle Assessment (LCA) techniques which are part of the ISO 14000 environmental management standards, namely ISO 14040:2006 and 14044:2006 which can help your business identify the overall impact of its products. The authors of the GHG Protocol, Carbon Trust and the WRI, are working on guidelines for life-cycle assessment of GHG emissions

more efficient product design, offering objects which perform better and with less energy, and which last longer before they need to be replaced. Obsolescence will become something to avoid, not a desirable feature built into a product to encourage bigger sales.

There is also a need for global solidarity to achieve climate neutrality. The developing countries do not need the developed countries' old, energy-hungry equipment, provided to them just because exporting it is an easier way to get rid of it and even makes some people feel virtuous. The climate diet will not work if inefficient devices remain in use. You will reduce your own emissions, yes, but at the cost of unnecessarily increasing someone else's. Better keep your old machine as long as it is worth it, then recycle it and buy a more efficient replacement. At the same time, in the developing world, do not encourage the use of old equipment, but support the introduction of the latest available technology worldwide.

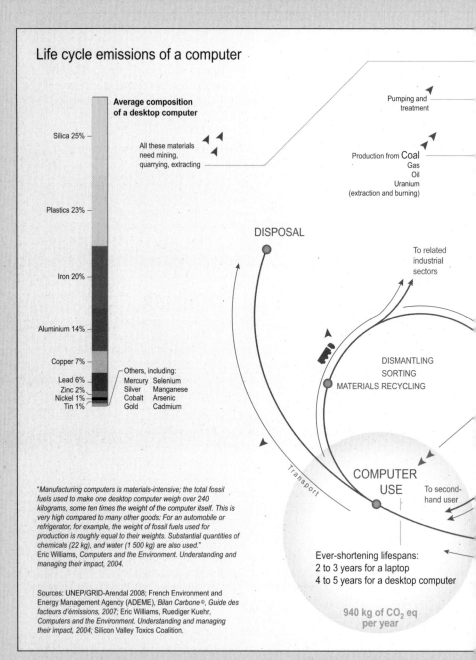

Life cycle emissions of a computer

Average composition of a desktop computer

Silica 25%

Plastics 23%

Iron 20%

Aluminium 14%

Copper 7%

Lead 6%
Zinc 2%
Nickel 1%
Tin 1%

Others, including:
Mercury   Selenium
Silver   Manganese
Cobalt   Arsenic
Gold   Cadmium

All these materials need mining, quarrying, extracting

Pumping and treatment

Production from **Coal**
Gas
Oil
Uranium
(extraction and burning)

DISPOSAL

To related industrial sectors

DISMANTLING
SORTING
MATERIALS RECYCLING

Transport

COMPUTER USE

To second-hand user

Ever-shortening lifespans:
2 to 3 years for a laptop
4 to 5 years for a desktop computer

940 kg of CO_2 eq per year

"Manufacturing computers is materials-intensive; the total fossil fuels used to make one desktop computer weigh over 240 kilograms, some ten times the weight of the computer itself. This is very high compared to many other goods: For an automobile or refrigerator, for example, the weight of fossil fuels used for production is roughly equal to their weights. Substantial quantities of chemicals (22 kg), and water (1 500 kg) are also used."
Eric Williams, Computers and the Environment. Understanding and managing their impact, 2004.

Sources: UNEP/GRID-Arendal 2008; French Environment and Energy Management Agency (ADEME), Bilan Carbone ®, Guide des facteurs d'émissions, 2007; Eric Williams, Ruediger Kuehr, Computers and the Environment. Understanding and managing their impact, 2004; Silicon Valley Toxics Coalition.

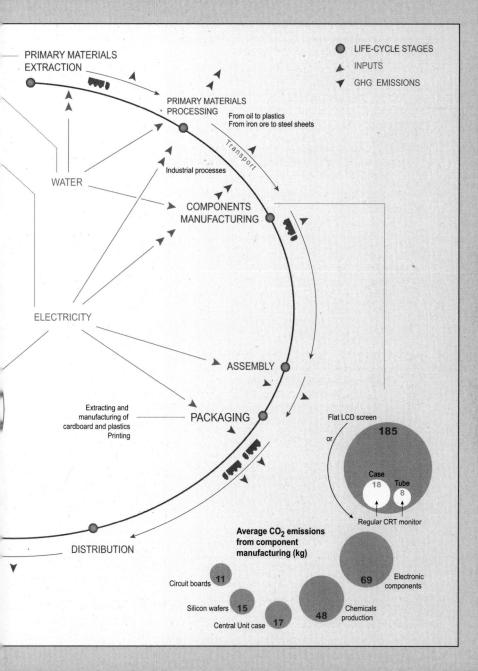

PRIMARY MATERIALS
EXTRACTION

PRIMARY MATERIALS
PROCESSING

From oil to plastics
From iron ore to steel sheets

Transport

WATER

Industrial processes

COMPONENTS
MANUFACTURING

ELECTRICITY

ASSEMBLY

Extracting and
manufacturing of
cardboard and plastics
Printing

PACKAGING

DISTRIBUTION

● LIFE-CYCLE STAGES
▲ INPUTS
▼ GHG EMISSIONS

Flat LCD screen

185

or

Case
18

Tube
8

Regular CRT monitor

**Average CO₂ emissions
from component
manufacturing (kg)**

Circuit boards **11**

Silicon wafers **15**

Central Unit case **17**

48

Chemicals
production

69

Electronic
components

Some examples of the effect of individual behaviour on greenhouse gas emissions in France

The area of the squares is proportionate to the annual reduction in emissions in million tonnes of CO_2 equivalent.

Housing
Investment

2,34 — Improving the insulation of an existing gas or oil-heated dwelling

Possible gain if rehabilitation (at a rate of 3% per annum) of France's 20.2 million gas or oil-heated dwellings improves insulation sufficiently to achieve annual energy consumption of 50 kWh per sq m, compared with 200 at present.

 0,26 — Building a new gas or oil-heated dwelling

Possible gain if the 130 000 new dwellings built on average every year, primarily heated using gas or oil, target annual energy consumption of 50 kWh per sq m, compared with 130 at present.

0,37 — Purchasing a new low-temperature or condensing boiler

Possible gain if all the 450 000 individual boilers replaced every year are high-performance boilers, compared with only 95 500 at present.

0,034 Fitting a solar-powered boiler

Possible gain if the goal of energy framework legislation to install 200 000 solar-powered boilers a year by 2010 is brought forward to 2005 and continued till 2020.

0,09 — Buying an energy class A+ household electrics appliance

Possible gain if all household electrical appliances replaced annually (9% of total) meet energy class A+ requirements, thus cutting energy consumption by 20%[1].

1. Relatively low gain as most electricity in France is nuclear-powered.

Daily life

7,7 — Lowering the inside temperature by 2°C in winter

Possible gain if the inside temperature of all dwellings is reduced by 2°C, corresponding to a 14% reduction in energy consumption.

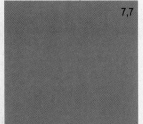

0,6 — Replacing conventional light bulbs with low-energy bulbs

Possible gain if all lighting is provided by low-energy light bulbs, which consume five times less energy than conventional bulbs.

3,5 — Regularly maintaining gas or oil-fuel boilers

Possible gain if gas or oil-fuel boilers are regularly maintained, improving overall efficiency by 5%, in the 15 million dwellings concerned.

0,08 Optimizing use of washing machine

Possible gain if all households use the cold-wash programme, thus saving 40% energy, at night, off-peak electricity production emitting less carbon.

Greenhouse gas emissions in France in 2004, by sector

563 million tonnes CO_2 equivalent

13%	14%	21%	18%	12%	13%	7%	2%
Housing	Individual road transport	Farming and agrifood	Manufacturing industry	Other transport including goods	Energy transf-ormation	Services, trade and institutions	Waste processing

Not including carbon sinks and biomass

Private car
Investment

Buying a new car that emits less than 120 g of CO_2 per km

0,8

Possible gain if the 2 million new vehicles purchased annually emit 120 g of CO_2 per km at the most (vehicles actually available) instead of 152 g per km, which is the average for new cars currently on the market.

Estimated values calculated by France's Environment Institute (Ifen), drawing on various sources: Manicore; Ceren; Ministry of Works statistics department (Sesp); Insee; Ademe; Environment Ministry (MIES), climate plan 2004; Enertech; Citepa; Energy Observatory.

Sources: Philippe Rekacewicz, *Atlas Environnement du Monde Diplomatique, 2007*; Florence Naizot and Patrice Grégoire, "Les ménages acteurs des émissions de gaz à effet de serre", Le 4 pages, n° 115, November-December 2006, Ifen.

Buying a second-hand car that uses less energy

1

Possible gain if among the 5.6 million second-hand cars purchased annually, buyers choose more recent vehicles for the same financial outlay (smaller, lighter, less powerful car in a lower price range).

Daily use

Cutting distance travelled annually by 10%

8,8

Possible gain if all households reduce travel, for instance by grouping short trips (shopping, school-run, services, etc.), changing means of transport (to walking, cycling or public transit), car-sharing or taking the train for long journeys previously made by car.

2,8

Driving more gently

Possible gain if all households adopt a greener style of driving for all trips (cutting down speed, not accelerating at obstacles, using gears to brake, keeping tyres fully inflated).

Reducing use of car air-conditioning

1,3

Maximum possible gain if use of air-conditioning is avoided in the 11.3 million equipped vehicles, its use increasing fuel consumption by 11 to 15%. Kept to a minimum, more modest use of air-conditioning is possible on a daily basis.

Use your common sense

You need to think of what will work for you. Solutions do not usually come in a one-size-fits-all format: they have to be tailored to individual circumstances. Perhaps you have a job which requires you to have a car always available. That cuts down your chances of reducing the energy you use in transport. Perhaps you care for an elderly relative who needs warmth: not much scope there for reducing your heating bills as much as you could otherwise. Choosing what will work for you, of course, goes hand-in-hand with a determination to make as many GHG savings as you can. So, if you cannot do much in one area, you will probably want to make bigger cuts in other areas. And the bottom line remains the same: usually, the more energy you save, the more money you will save too.

● INDIVIDUALS

For many individuals in industrialized countries, food and related services make up the biggest chunk of emissions related to goods. Getting started on this is not too complicated. Buying only the food we need means refrigerators working less hard, less food being wasted and **thrown away,** less

Freeganism is a movement of mostly middle-class urban American – and increasingly global – anti-consumerists who, among other radical acts of refusal to subdue themselves to the dominant economic laws of our societies, feed themselves on meals prepared from food found in urban waste bins. Freegans do not do so out of pure necessity, but to draw attention to the excesses of our throw-away culture. And not only that: by recovering discards from retailers, offices, schools, homes, hotels, or anywhere else, by rummaging through their trash bins, dumpsters, and trash bags, freegans are able to obtain food, beverages, books, toiletries magazines, comic books, newspapers, videos, kitchenware, appliances, music (CDs, cassettes, records, etc.), carpets, musical instruments, clothing, rollerblades, scooters, furniture, vitamins, electronics, animal care products, games, toys, bicycles, artwork, and just about any other type of consumer goods. Rather than contributing to further waste, freegans curtail garbage and pollution, reducing the overall volume of the waste stream. www.freegan.info.

energy being wasted on producing the food and transporting it to our tables. And for those with a garden, how about the revolutionary idea of growing some of our own food? Without necessarily going all the way and installing a pig in every household, or even a few chickens, home-grown food will probably be fresher, taste better and do you more good than what you can buy in the shops. And it will take minimal energy – except your own – to grow it. Comparing emissions from meat production with growing vegetables shows that part of the answer clearly lies in eating more plant material and less meat and processed food. Similarly, wearing clothes until the end of their useful lives – even mending them when they need it – uses much less energy than always being in the vanguard of fashion.

Perhaps it would be helpful here to recap some of the ways you can cut your emissions without having to influence anyone apart from yourself – perhaps on a typical weekday.

You wake up, thrust rudely into consciousness by your electric alarm: time to look out the old wind-up alarm clock which was good enough for your grandparents, and which needed no external energy source to keep it going. By the way, how warm is your bedroom overnight? Would an extra blanket or a thicker duvet let you reduce the temperature by a few degrees? You head for the bathroom: how much energy you use depends on the length and temperature of your shower. You can blow-dry your hair, or just leave it to dry naturally. **Breakfast** is modest, but boiling water (just enough)

The food industry is one of the most GHG-intensive sectors when you factor in the supply chain and the impact of agricultural production (see the Climate Action Programme: www.climateactionprogramme.org). Eating less meat and dairy products makes for more efficient food production. Meat takes more energy because it takes longer to produce, and animals are inefficient converters of grain. They need to be fed on farmed plant products which could feed many more people directly. Manure releases methane, and so do ruminants like cows, as the food ferments in their stomachs. That is why becoming a vegetarian will not help if you simply replace animal proteins with dairy products. Dairy cows produce over twice as much methane as beef cattle. However, sustainable meat production is possible: it involves grazing that improves soil quality, makes biogas which can be used as renewable energy, and avoids energy intensive activities. Organic farming avoids the use of fossil fuel-based fertilizers and keeps the soil in good shape. But organic food may not manage to feed the world; partly because of the space it requires.

Look at the entire production and supply chain when you are thinking what to buy and cook. Buying raw ingredients and cooking your own food instead of buying processed food saves the energy used for packaging, chilling and storing ready meals. And when it comes to disposal, composting reduces GHGs.

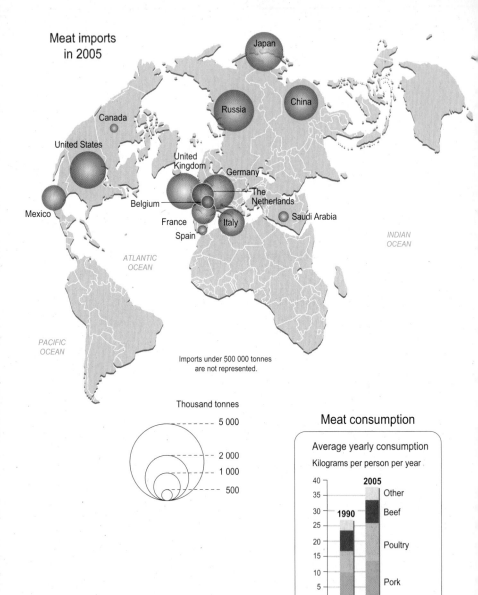

Meat imports
in 2005

Japan

China

Russia

Canada

United States

United
Kingdom

Germany

The
Netherlands

Belgium

Mexico

France

Italy

Saudi Arabia

Spain

INDIAN
OCEAN

ATLANTIC
OCEAN

PACIFIC
OCEAN

Imports under 500 000 tonnes
are not represented.

Thousand tonnes

5 000

2 000

1 000

500

Meat consumption

Average yearly consumption
Kilograms per person per year

2005

40

35

Other

30

Beef

25

1990

20

Poultry

15

10

5

Pork

0

Source: Food and Agriculture Organization of the United Nations, 2007.

Animal proteins:
the good, the bad and the ugly

Kilograms of CO_2 equivalents
per 100 kilocalories of product

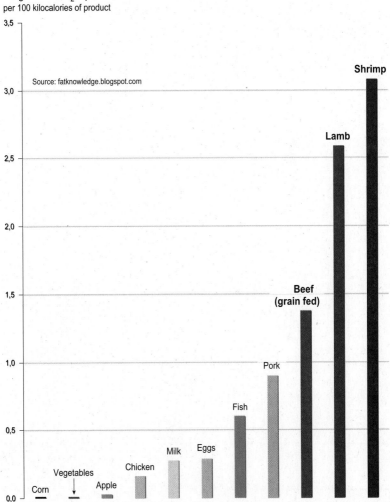

Source: fatknowledge.blogspot.com

Shrimp

Lamb

Beef
(grain fed)

Pork

Fish

Eggs

Milk

Chicken

Corn

Vegetables

Apple

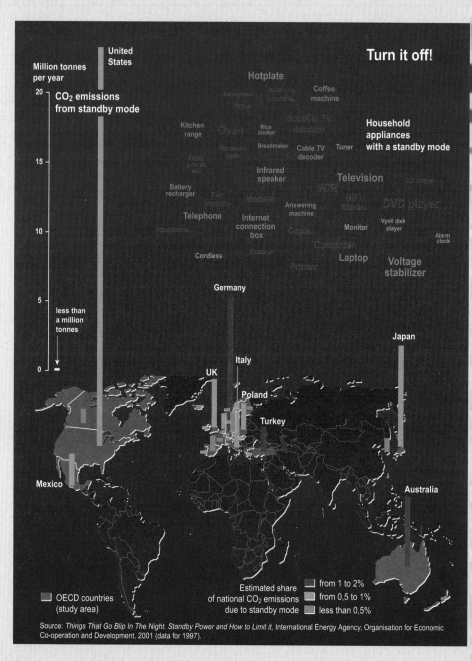

Turn it off!

Million tonnes per year

CO₂ emissions from standby mode

Household appliances with a standby mode

Hotplate · Coffee machine · Refrigerator · Washing machine · Stove · Kitchen range · Oven · Rice cooker · Satellite TV decoder · Microwave oven · Breadmaker · Cable TV decoder · Tuner · Video games set · Infrared speaker · Television · CD player · Battery recharger · VCR · HIFI Stereo · DVD player · Fax machine · Modem · Answering machine · Telephone · Internet connection box · Copier · Monitor · Vynil disk player · Alarm clock · Interphone · Cordless · Scanner · Computer · Laptop · Voltage stabilizer · Printer

United States

Germany

Italy

UK

Poland

Turkey

Japan

Mexico

Australia

less than a million tonnes

OECD countries (study area)

Estimated share of national CO₂ emissions due to standby mode

from 1 to 2%
from 0,5 to 1%
less than 0,5%

Source: *Things That Go Blip In The Night. Standby Power and How to Limit it,* International Energy Agency, Organisation for Economic Co-operation and Development, 2001 (data for 1997).

for your tea in an electric kettle uses half the energy your stove takes. Do you toast a slice of bread from a loaf or have a part-baked croissant which demands more energy to heat it? Then there's your **fridge**: is it rated A+ or

> *Energy-hungry household appliances account for GHG emissions both in use and during their production. Before buying, investigate different models and choose the most efficient. Choose to pay more for quality that promises to last – you will get a better deal than if you buy a cheaper model which you have to replace three times. If it breaks, try to have it repaired before replacing it (see the calculations of efficiency versus manufacturing emissions). Energy efficiency labels are useful but sometimes misleading. They will tell you the appliance's relative efficiency for its size, but you would do better to take into account its absolute efficiency. The biggest users of electricity in the average household are tumble dryers, refrigerators and freezers, washing machines and televisions. And they are not always essential: do you really need a tumble dryer, or could you manage with a clothes line?*

A++ for its energy efficiency? How do you clean your teeth – with an electric or a manual toothbrush?

You commute to the office: do you use your car or the subway? And at work, a flat-screen monitor and laptop use less power than desktops and cathode ray tubes. Lunch next. If you choose meat, that will normally have taken more energy to reach your plate than vegetables or pasta. (Meanwhile, are you sure you have not left your computer – or any other appliance – on **standby** in your office?) After work you have a quick snack,

> *The International Energy Agency estimates that standby mode could be causing a full 1 per cent of world's greenhouse gas emissions, close to what the entire aviation industry emits. Standby power consumption for most devices is small – typically ranging from 0.5 to 15 watts but the number of devices drawing standby power is large. A European, Japanese, Australian, or North American home often contains 20 devices constantly drawing standby power. A standard TV set, DVD or CD player wastes up to 50 per cent of the energy it consumes while in stand-by mode. As a result, standby power is responsible for 5–10 per cent of total electricity use in most homes and an unknown amount in commercial buildings and factories.*
>
> *A simple way to reduce power consumption and the resulting emissions is to use a multi-plug rail with a power switch and turn it off over night. A complementary approach is for industry to aim at reducing electricity consumption in new appliances when they are on stand-by. The IEA has launched a campaign aiming to reduce stand-by consumption to one watt. www.iea.org/textbase/papers/2005/standby_fact.pdf.*

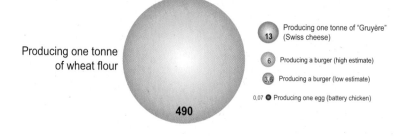

Producing one tonne of wheat flour **490**

13 Producing one tonne of "Gruyère" (Swiss cheese)

6 Producing a burger (high estimate)

3,6 Producing a burger (low estimate)

0,07 ● Producing one egg (battery chicken)

perhaps some **strawberries.** If they were imported by air from South Af-

Food is one of the most transported goods in our globalized world and we have grown used to seeing strawberries almost all year round in our supermarkets. In the US food travels on average 1 300 to 2 000 miles (2 100 to 3 200 kilometres) before it reaches the consumer. To tackle the issue of food miles movements have developed across the world to protest at this long journey. One of them is "The 100-Mile Diet". As the name suggests, it urges the buying and eating of food that has been grown, manufactured or produced entirely within a 100-mile radius of your home. This is one way people can reduce their carbon footprint while supporting local food. Another term that has become very fashionable in this context is "locavores", the American "word of the year" in 2007. It is a combination of the Latin words "localis" and "devorare" – "local" and "devour" – and promotes the consumption of locally grown and produced food.

The second largest Swiss supermarket chain recently proudly announced the launch of a little airplane sticker on products that travelled by air, in order to raise customers' awareness of the CO_2 emissions involved and to give them the opportunity to limit their own climate footprint by avoiding the products if they wished. But distance travelled is not the only factor in a product's CO_2 balance. To make sure you are really improving your climate balance you need to look at the entire production and supply chain. For instance a recent study showed that tomatoes grown in Spain and transported to the United Kingdom may have a lower carbon footprint in terms of energy efficiency than tomatoes grown in the UK itself, because of the energy needed to heat greenhouses there.

rica they will have taken almost 6 kg of CO_2 to reach you. But if they came by lorry from Italy, they will account for much less than 0.25 kg. Then it is time for sport: you could go jogging on a treadmill at a fitness centre, but why not save energy by simply running in the park? You do some shopping on the way home. Are you concerned to choose food that is in season, has not had to be kept frozen for months and is not **over-packed** in climate-

> Reducing GHG emissions from waste is about capturing methane generated in the landfill through the decomposition of organic materials such as food scraps, garden waste and paper. Sewage and wastewater treatment plants also release methane when they break down waste.
>
> Reduction of GHG emissions from waste can be achieved by utilising the anaerobic digestion (AD) process caused by bacteria in the absence of oxygen, for biogas production. Biogas consists mainly of methane (around 60 per cent) and CO_2 (around 40 per cent) (with traces of hydrogen sulphide and ammonia). The process is exactly the same as occurs in the landfill anyway, but under controlled conditions. The biogas can be used for electricity and heat generation. The main limitations of such a process are high capital and operating costs, especially at large scales. Successful energy generation depends on providing a continuous supply, adequate storage and reduced transport requirements (so the schemes should be mainly local).
>
> In theory, well-managed waste incineration plants and biogas production from disposal sites are valuable energy sources. But the technology needs to be applied more widely until uncontrolled dumps disappear. What is more worrying is excessive waste generation itself: finite resources are transformed into single-use, GHG-emitting goods that all too quickly end up in landfills.

hostile material? Home for dinner, and you may decide it is simpler and quicker to thaw some frozen vegetables, instead of cooking fresh ones on the stove. Doing the laundry means still more decisions: do you use a high temperature wash or choose a lower one that takes less power? Do you use the tumble dryer or leave the washing to dry on a clothesline? The evening is for watching TV. Hopefully it has not been on stand-by all day long, together with the DSL modem, the DVD player and the stereo. Before bed you check your emails: perhaps you have read the warning from one industry figure, that worldwide internet usage alone needs the equivalent of 14 power stations for the necessary computers and servers.

The net result of the exercise is perhaps surprising. Someone who does not think about the climate impact of the way they live would be responsible for emissions of about 38 kg of CO_2 for a day like this. Yet somebody who thought hard could enjoy virtually the same level of comfort for a much more modest CO_2 burden of 14 kg. Often that is all it takes – a conscious effort to think about the impact we are having.

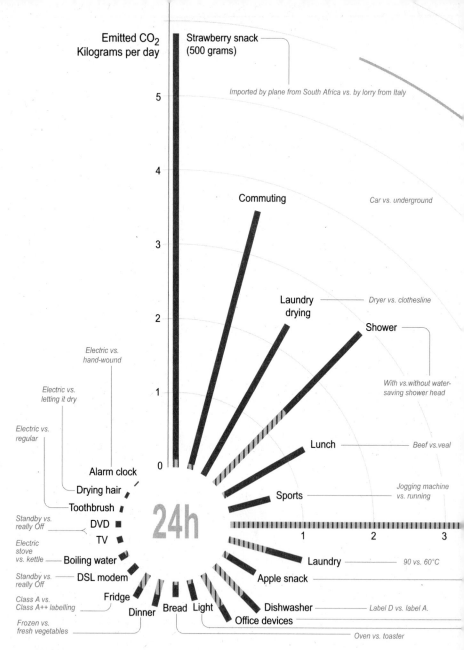

Emitted CO$_2$
Kilograms per day

Strawberry snack
(500 grams)

Imported by plane from South Africa vs. by lorry from Italy

Commuting

Car vs. underground

Laundry
drying

Dryer vs. clothesline

Shower

With vs. without water-saving shower head

Lunch

Beef vs. veal

Sports

Jogging machine vs. running

*Electric vs.
hand-wound*

*Electric vs.
letting it dry*

*Electric vs.
regular*

Alarm clock

Drying hair

Toothbrush

DVD

TV

Boiling water

DSL modem

Fridge

Dinner

Bread

Light

24h

Laundry

90 vs. 60°C

Apple snack

Dishwasher

Label D vs. label A.

Office devices

*Standby vs.
really Off*

*Electric
stove
vs. kettle*

*Standby vs.
really Off*

*Class A vs.
Class A++ labelling*

*Frozen vs.
fresh vegetables*

Oven vs. toaster

Same comfort level, same needs, different choices

In this example, CO_2 emitted each day by two persons living in Munich are detailed, showing two different ways of fulfilling the same needs: 38 kg of CO_2 emitted by an average consumer versus 14 kg by a more aware one.

CO_2 emitted by a regular consumer

The difference represents CO_2 emissions that can be avoided without losing much comfort.

CO_2 emitted by a "climate-conscious" consumer

Sorted from the biggest to the smallest difference between the two consumers

With vs. without cooler (a few degrees colder)

Source: Nadeschda Scharfenberg, Süddeutsche Zeitung, March 10, 2007 (primary sources: Deutsche Energie-Agentur, BUND, Bayerisches Umweltministerium, Münchner Verkehrsgesellschaft, Volkswagen, Kettler.)

Heating

5   6   7   8   9   10

Imported by boat from New Zealand vs. by lorry from Bavaria

On vs. Off at night and during lunch hour

Regular vs. energy-saving bulbs

Note: calculation is based on an average household, where one kilowatt per hour accounts for 530 grams of CO_2.
This value can be improved by using renewable energy sources for electricity production.

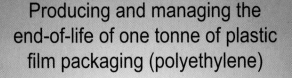

Manufacturing
a computer
and a monitor

275

Producing and managing the
end-of-life of one tonne of plastic
film packaging (polyethylene)

6 480

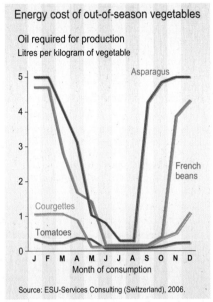

Energy cost of out-of-season vegetables

Oil required for production
Litres per kilogram of vegetable

Asparagus

French beans

Courgettes

Tomatoes

5 4 3 2 1 0

J F M A M J J A S O N D
Month of consumption

Source: ESU-Services Consulting (Switzerland), 2006.

Consumer power can work, and so can the power of those determined to consume less or consume in a smarter way. And the choices you make about what you consume will eventually filter through to affect business and industry. You are one individual, but the decisions you make allow you to wield power on a wider stage. If products are made to last, do not replace them. If they are not, do not buy them – and tell the manufacturer why you are choosing something else.

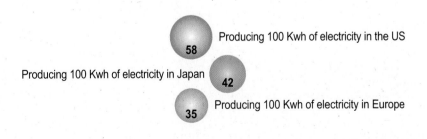

58 Producing 100 Kwh of electricity in the US

Producing 100 Kwh of electricity in Japan **42**

35 Producing 100 Kwh of electricity in Europe

Companies and other organizations – including NGOs – are producers but also major buyers of goods and services, and can direct their purchasing power to move markets towards more climate-friendly products. A growing number of companies, universities, government departments and other groups now have formal purchasing policies that encourage or sometimes require staff responsible for spending decisions to choose the **greener options** avail-

Green procurement means a conscious buying policy based on ecological principles, where financial aspects alone do not determine the choice of one product over another, or where a contract is given not to the lowest bidder but to the one with the least impact on the environment. Higher purchasing prices are in many cases compensated by lower operating costs. Many city and business administrations have turned to green procurement policies in the process of introducing sustainable management systems. Public procurement accounts for 16 per cent of EU GDP, so greening public procurement can become a powerful economic driver for environmental technologies. A guide to green procurement for public authorities is available in 22 languages from the EU: http://ec.europa.eu/environment/gpp/guideline_en.htm. Their recommendations are:

- Purchase green products (recycled, refurbished, or reconditioned products that are competitive in price, performance and quality with new ones); rent or lease equipment instead of buying.
- Pursue electricity/energy from renewable sources – checking with energy-supplying companies for "green energy" arrangements.
- Green company fleet – purchase or lease vehicles with the highest possible fuel economy, or that use alternative sources of energy like electricity, fuel cells or hybrids.

able. Engaging in green procurement means matching conventional performance requirements with environmental ones. This often requires finding new vendors. Some climate-neutral products and services cost more than their conventional counterparts. Using them will probably involve rethinking ingrained habits. But the potential gains are often longer lifetimes and lower running costs.

80

Running all kitchen appliances for a year (rich countries)

For *industries*, specifically those in Asia, there is a website that offers

Industry accounts for about a quarter of global GHG emissions and most of these come from the use of fossil fuels for energy generation or from direct production of CO_2 as part of processing, for instance during cement production. Almost all the GHG emissions from this sector (20 per cent including emissions from the power sector, or 14 per cent without it) come from a small group of energy-intensive industries such as iron and steel, chemicals and fertilizers, cement, glass and ceramics, pulp and paper. Solutions can be found in familiar buzz words like energy efficiency measures and carbon capture and storage, but these emissions need tackling seriously. We have to rethink not only the way they are produced but also the consumption of the resulting products, which is where almost everyone can contribute. Just think about how you are directly and indirectly demanding the products listed above.

help to companies which want to improve energy efficiency through cleaner production and to stakeholders who want to help them. It is the *Energy Efficiency Guide for Industry in Asia*, at www.energyefficiencyasia. org. The guide includes a methodology, case studies for more than 40 Asian companies in five industry sectors, technical information for 25 types of energy equipment, training materials, and a contact and information database.

Although the site (developed by UNEP and others) is described as being for Asian industry, much of what it says will be applicable far beyond the continent. It contains a wealth of material, aimed at managers, production staff, suppliers, customers, research institutes and universities, financial institutions, NGOs and even governments. Specific industries covered are pulp and paper, ceramics, chemicals, cement, and iron and steel. The material is available in English and in several Asian languages.

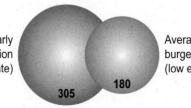

Average American yearly burger consumption (high estimate)

Average American yearly burger consumption (low estimate)

305

180

Largest industrial CO$_2$ emitters

Facilities emitting more
than 100 000 tonnes of CO$_2$ each year

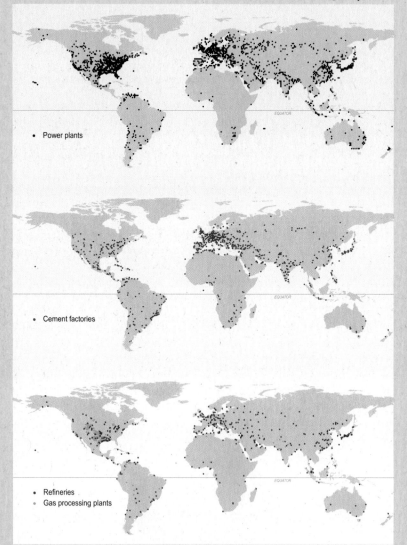

- Power plants

- Cement factories

- Refineries
- Gas processing plants

EQUATOR

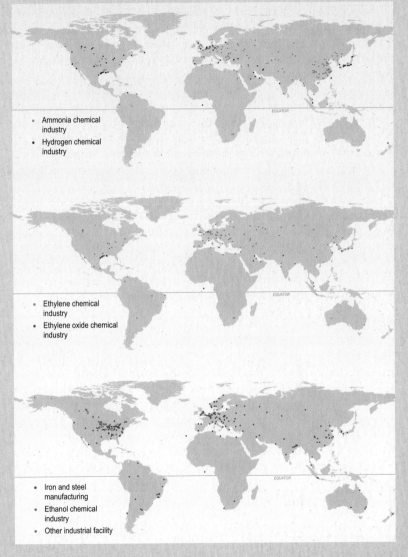

Cities can exert an influence reducing climate impacts in at least two ways. They are responsible for making sure that in their own administration and activities (their governance role) they are moving towards climate-neutrality as fast as they can. They also influence their citizens' and other actors' behaviour, for example industry and transport. This is their role as players in the community. So they can motivate others and enlist them to take part in reducing emissions.

There is plenty individual cities can do to work towards climate neutrality. Just like companies, they can make sure their procurement policies are helping. Where public procurement is concerned, city administrations are big buyers of materials and equipment: paper, computers, furniture, vehicle fleets (not only cars and buses but waste collection vehicles, ambulances, fire engines and so forth).

They are also responsible for equipping public buildings and spaces. Here they can be careful always to apply climate-friendly criteria, for example when it comes to material choices and energy demand. Cities can also make sure their procurement policies specify the use of organic and local food and drinks in cafeterias, schools, city-run operas and theatres, and every other institution for which they are responsible.

Walking the talk

The Swedish city of Växjö – one of the founder members of UNEP's Climate Neutral Network – proclaims itself the Greenest City in Europe. Its CO_2 emissions fell by 30 per cent per capita between 1993 and 2006. In absolute terms, every citizen of Växjö contributes 3.2 tonnes of CO_2 to the atmosphere, far below the European (EU25 in 2000) average of around 8.5 tonnes per person. The city has achieved this result largely by virtue of the large share of biomass used for heating. Nearly 90 per cent of Växjö's heating comes from renewable sources. Most current emissions come from transport, but this sector has also seen a decrease lately, thanks to increasing numbers of environment-friendly vehicles and greater use of biofuel.

Another innovator is the Dutch city of The Hague, which uses seawater to heat houses. The system extracts seawater and then processes it via either a heat exchanger or a heat pump (depending on the time of year) to supply an entire residential area with space heating and hot water. The energy yield produced by drawing heat from the sea is 1 100 per cent, and that in turn results in a 50 per cent reduction in CO_2 emissions. Users pay no more for this system than for a conventional one.

Engaging others

There are other ways of saving energy. The city council of Freiburg in Germany permits the construction only of low energy buildings on municipal land, and all new buildings must meet low energy specifications. Low energy housing uses solar power passively as well as actively. Besides solar panels and collectors on the roof, which provide electricity and hot water, many passive features of the houses use solar energy for regulating room temperature. Freiburg's solar policy embraces the entire city. Various companies and public facilities make their roofs available for solar panels, in which the people of Freiburg can buy shares. They are paid for the power sold to the municipal electricity scheme.

The British town of Stretton is providing its citizens with climate change classes to show the 5 000 households how they can reduce their climate footprint. The classes are based on the idea of a slimming club. A computer programme will calculate how much GHG emissions each household is responsible for and then suggest ways of reducing that weight with participants invited back later for an emissions "weigh-in". They will learn how high their emissions are through a computer programme which will also suggest ways of reducing that "weight".

Joining forces

C40 (www.c40cities.org) is a group of the world's largest cities, all of them committed to tackling climate change. Cities are central to the task, particularly as they bear a disproportionate responsibility for causing the problem. Cities consume 75 per cent of the world's energy and produce 80 per cent of its greenhouse gas emissions. One idea promoted by C40 is the potential of cities to do more together than they can on their own. Pooling their buying power can bring down the prices of energy-saving products and speed the development and uptake of new energy-saving technologies. A consortium being developed by C40's partner, the Clinton Climate Initiative, will form partnerships with vendors that will lead to lower production and delivery costs and therefore lower prices. Key product categories will include building materials, systems, and controls; traffic and street lighting; clean buses and waste disposal trucks; and waste-to-energy systems.

ICLEI (Local Governments for Sustainability) runs a campaign called *Cities for Climate Protection (CCP)*. It helps cities adopt policies and implement quantifiable measures to reduce local greenhouse gas emissions, improve air quality, and enhance urban liveability and sustainability. More than 800 local governments participate in the CCP, integrating climate change mitigation into their decision-making processes. Five milestones help local governments to understand how municipal decisions affect energy use and how these decisions can be used to mitigate global climate change while improving the community's quality of life. Like the generic environmental management system (EMS) approach, the CCP methodology provides a simple, standardized way of acting to reduce GHGs emissions and monitoring, measuring, and reporting performance.

COUNTRIES

Decisions taken at country level can influence and motivate actors ranging from the international community to individuals and have a profound effect on GHG emissions and patterns of consumption and production. Whereas cities are in a better position to motivate people and unlock their enthusiasm, countries have the power to induce fundamental changes. One way of motivating people is by offering them ways to save money, yet not all governments have exploited the potential of the taxation system to change behaviour to greener patterns. Governments can, for example, introduce carbon taxes on the use of fossil fuels. They can impose taxes on the extraction and production of minerals, energy and timber and structure them to support more climate-friendly practices. Specific taxes are possible on technologies and products which cause significant environmental damage. Waste disposal, pollution and hazardous wastes can also be taxed. To compensate taxpayers for these new impositions governments can lower other charges, for instance income and sales taxes, and those on property and investment, or simply pay back the amount equally to every inhabitant, as is done in Switzerland with the CO$_2$ **tax** on fossil heating fuels. At the

> Germany has introduced several eco-taxes. The first was on electricity and petrol, at variable rates based on environmental factors; renewable electricity is not taxed. The second adjusted taxes to favour efficient conventional power plants, and the third increased the petrol tax. At the same time, income taxes were reduced proportionally so that the total tax burden remained constant. This is a crucial issue in countries where citizens have a say on taxation. Often, a law will not pass if it implies additional funds for the state. But if it is income-neutral and only penalises those who pollute more to reward the ones who pollute less, there is a higher chance that the new law will pass.

same time revenue can be used to create incentives and compensate those companies who invest in climate friendly alternatives.

But not everybody is convinced that taxing environmentally-unfriendly products or activities is the way forward. Mark Moody-Stuart, ex-chairman of Shell, told the London *Times* that merely taxing "gas-guzzling" cars allowed the rich to evade responsibility for climate change: "When we eliminated coal fires in London we didn't say to people in Chelsea you can pay a bit more and toast your crumpets in front of an open fire. We said nobody could have an open fire."

New Zealand, one of the founder members of the UNEP Climate Neutral Network, has a public information site (www.sustainability.govt.nz) to enlist and encourage everyone concerned to reduce their footprint. Leading by example, its Carbon Neutral Public Sector Initiative seeks to demonstrate the Government's leadership on sustainability and achieving climate neutrality. The programme aims to offset the GHG emissions of an initial group of six governmental agencies by 2012. Unavoidable emissions will be offset, primarily through indigenous forest regeneration projects on conservation land. All 34 public service agencies were due to have emission reduction plans in place by December 2007.

How we move

Mobility is getting cheaper for many people (though not everyone) in industrial countries, often so cheap that we scarcely notice the cost. For the atmosphere, though, the price is getting higher all the time, because most methods of transport involve high greenhouse gas emissions. Aircraft are usually the most polluting. Trains are always the ***preferable option*** climate-wise and also time-wise

Flying is one of the most dominant topics when it comes to the villains of climate change, but looking at the sober facts, its overall contribution to global CO_2 emissions is not striking. According to the WRI, about 1.5 % of global GHG emissions are generated by flying. But aviation is a fast-growing contributor to climate change. What counts is not only the CO_2 emissions but also ozone generation through nitrogen oxide emissions and the formation of condensation trails, so-called contrails, from water vapour release which also have warming effects. The IPCC estimates the overall impact of an aircraft on the climate is about two to four times higher than the impact of its CO_2 emissions alone and concludes that aviation is responsible for around 3.5% of anthropogenic climate change, a figure which includes both CO_2 and non-CO_2 induced effects. It is important to remember this when comparing the climate performance of planes and ground transport modes.

Do you really save time?
Train versus plane in a busy world

Schedules — Train Plane

Selected routes →	New York Washington D.C.		Tokyo Osaka		Paris London		Hamburg München	
Flying distance →	330 km		405 km		340 km		610 km	
Departure from city centre	7hr00m	7hr00m	7hr00m	7hr00m	7hr00m	7hr00m	7hr00m	7hr00m
Arrival at airport		7hr20m		7hr35m		7hr45m		7hr40m
Check-in		7hr30m		7hr45m	7hr00m	8hr00m		8hr00m
Take-off / Departure		9hr00m		8hr45m	7hr30m	9hr00m		9hr15m
Landing		10hr25m		10hr05m		10hr10m		10hr30m
Baggage claim		10hr40m		10hr20m		10hr25m		10hr45m
Arrival in city centre	9hr35	11hr05m	9hr36m	10hr50m	9hr45m	11hr00m	12hr40m	11hr15m
Total travel time	2hr35	4hr05m	2hr35m	3hr50m	2hr45m	3hr00m	5hr40m	4hr15m
CO_2 emissions (kg)	**29**	**109**	**20**	**119**	**5,5**	**107**	**33**	**150**

White circles are proportional to emissions.

Eurostar (Channel Tunnel Train) plans to cut emissions by 25% per traveller journey by 2012

Even in this case where flying is faster, these are 5hr40m during which you can relax, work or sleep without interruption.

Sources: nyctourist.com, eurostar.com; amtrak.com; myclimate.org; bahn.de; www.amadeus.net; japanrail.com; www.keikyu.co.jp; aeroportsdeparis.fr.

they can often be a good alternative, capable of competing on time for distances of up to 800 kilometres or so once you include the time spent getting to and

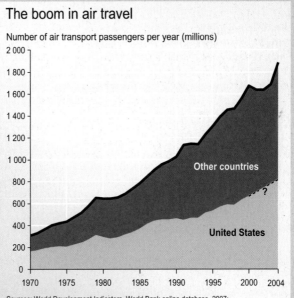

The boom in air travel

Number of air transport passengers per year (millions)

Other countries

United States

?

Sources: World Development Indicators, World Bank online database, 2007; International Civil Aviation Organization, 2006.

In most cases, trains are the preferred option for travelling in the most climate-friendly way. How much they actually save depends on how many people are on the train and what energy source it uses. Trains in Switzerland for example run on electricity from a mix of hydroelectric and nuclear power. In Norway they use 95 per cent hydroelectric power. In France, trains run on nuclear power, as most of the country's electricity is nuclear-based.

Europe has probably the most elaborate transnational train network in the world, but also a wide range of low-cost airlines offering cheap fares and frequent departures to numerous destinations. Apart from the price of a ticket, complicated connections and sometimes unfavourable timetables often put planes ahead in competing for customers.

To improve their services seven European high-speed rail operators have founded Railteam with the aim of offering integrated high-speed rail travel between major European cities and competing with airlines on punctuality, pricing and speed. The launch of a consistent ticketing system on a single website is planned for 2009.

from the airport instead of a city-centre railway station. Over short distances air travel produces around three times more CO_2 per passenger than rail. It is estimated to account for around 2–3 per cent of global CO_2 emissions and faces intense pressure to cap its output. However, it should not be denied that some of the new high-speed rail services have an appreciable carbon footprint themselves. Another good option for international or intercity travel may be a coach or bus, certainly better than a car carrying only one person. Within towns and cities buses outperform cars again, but they are seldom as good as trams, light rail systems or metros. Cycling and walking will always be the greenest ways of moving around a city, but not necessarily the safest, quickest or most practicable, which understandably makes many people reluctant to try them. That is where urban planners and politicians can make all the difference – by breaking with the dominance of cars in city streets and providing favourable conditions for alternative modes of transport. Having biking lanes and a working public transport system in place is one thing, the other is how useful they are. Urban planning can work towards a more functional and hence a more attractive transport system. Locating shopping malls for example in places where they can be easily reached by public transport is a strategy followed by Norway recently.

Shipping had been thought to be one of the better forms of transport for keeping GHGs down, but studies show that its global CO_2 emissions are double those of aviation, and rising rapidly. The IMO estimates shipping emissions at almost three per cent of global CO_2 emissions in 2007. Recent articles in the press suggests that CO_2 emissions from shipping have been grossly underestimated and would amount to 1 120 million tonnes or nearly 4.5 per cent of global CO_2 emissions. This is almost twice the UK's total emissions and exceeds all of Africa's.

The worldwide fleet of 90,000 ships transports 90 percent of the world's goods, and shipping emissions are projected to grow by more than 70 percent by 2020, as global trade expands. In order to tackle those emissions, the European Commission has decided to propose adding shipping companies to the EU Emissions Trading System from which shipping (just as aviation) has been exempted so far. The emissions trading scheme is the 27-nation EU's key tool to fight global warming and meet commitments to reduce emissions of greenhouse gases agreed under the Kyoto Protocol.

There are several ways of reducing the energy we use in travel and transport. One is to obtain what we use and consume as locally as possible, whether

Most commonly used air routes, in million passengers a year

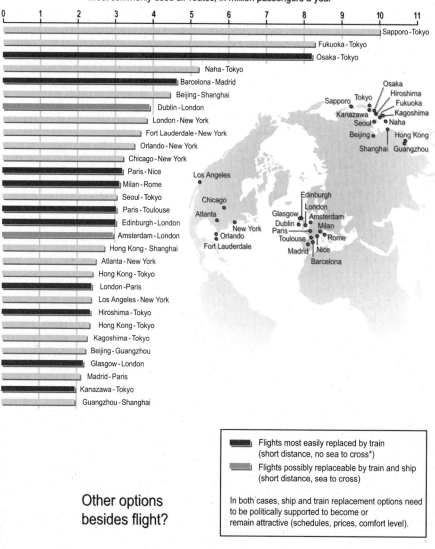

Most commonly used air routes (million passengers a year):
- Sapporo - Tokyo
- Fukuoka - Tokyo
- Osaka - Tokyo
- Naha - Tokyo
- Barcelona - Madrid
- Beijing - Shanghai
- Dublin - London
- London - New York
- Fort Lauderdale - New York
- Orlando - New York
- Chicago - New York
- Paris - Nice
- Milan - Rome
- Seoul - Tokyo
- Paris - Toulouse
- Edinburgh - London
- Amsterdam - London
- Hong Kong - Shanghai
- Atlanta - New York
- Hong Kong - Tokyo
- London - Paris
- Los Angeles - New York
- Hiroshima - Tokyo
- Hong Kong - Tokyo
- Kagoshima - Tokyo
- Beijing - Guangzhou
- Glasgow - London
- Madrid - Paris
- Kanazawa - Tokyo
- Guangzhou - Shanghai

Other options besides flight?

Legend:
- ▬▬ Flights most easily replaced by train (short distance, no sea to cross*)
- ▬▬ Flights possibly replaceable by train and ship (short distance, sea to cross)

In both cases, ship and train replacement options need to be politically supported to become or remain attractive (schedules, prices, comfort level).

* Given the Channel Tunnel train, London-Paris is counted in this category.
Source: ENAC Air Transport Database, French Civil Aviation University, 2008 (data for 2006).

Vancouver

Long Beach

Houston

New York

Pacific
Ocean

Saõ Paulo

Saõ Sebastiao

Tubarao

• Major merchandise port

—— Major shipping routes

••••••••• Projected shipping routes

Sources: John Vidal, "*Shipping boom fuels rising tide of global CO_2 emissions*", The Guardian, February 13 2008; *Atlas du Monde Diplomatique 2006*, Armand Colin; *Panorama des ports de commerce mondiaux 2003*, ISEMAR, January 2005; *Images économiques du monde 2002*, Sedes.

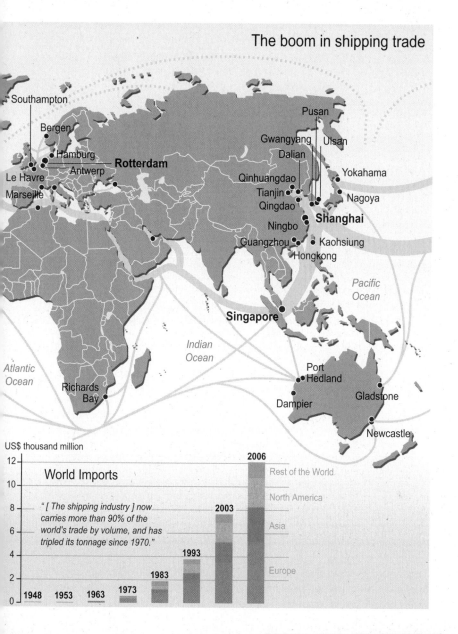

The boom in shipping trade

Southampton
Bergen
Hamburg
Rotterdam
Antwerp
Le Havre
Marseille

Pusan
Gwangyang Ulsan
Dalian
Qinhuangdao
Tianjin Yokahama
Qingdao Nagoya
Ningbo **Shanghai**
Guangzhou Kaohsiung
Hongkong

Pacific Ocean

Singapore

Indian Ocean

Atlantic Ocean

Richards Bay

Port Hedland
Dampier
Gladstone
Newcastle

US$ thousand million

World Imports

"[The shipping industry] now carries more than 90% of the world's trade by volume, and has tripled its tonnage since 1970."

12
10
8
6
4
2
0

1948 1953 1963 1973 1983 1993 2003 2006

Rest of the World
North America
Asia
Europe

food, clothing or even work: in most industrialized countries, commuting accounts for much of the energy used in moving around. Another is to improve the efficiency of the vehicles that are used for transporting people or goods. Airbus, which builds the super-jumbo A380 aircraft, says the industry's performance on **fuel consumption** is twice as good as in 1960, and the A380

> Compared with ground vehicles, the prospect for replacing kerosene in aircraft engines with low carbon alternatives looks far more difficult, from a technological and economic perspective. Potential alternatives must meet high demands: supporting extreme cold, lightweight and low cost (kerosene not being subject to taxation) among others.
>
> Meanwhile engineers and airlines are focussing on improved energy efficiency mainly through better engines, lighter materials, increased capacity and lower fuel consumption (by improving air traffic management and energy-saving flying techniques).
>
> To apply market rules and adjust the price of air travel to the impact it generates, making other means of transport more attractive at the same time, is another option for reducing emissions. Although emissions from aviation, just as from shipping, are exempted from the Kyoto Protocol in any country's emission target, the European Commission has adopted a proposal to include aviation in the EU Emissions Trading Scheme (ETS) from 2011. For the post-Kyoto agreement after 2012, the inclusion of aviation emissions could be one of the political solutions.
>
> In 2006 the Scandinavian airline SAS began testing a new landing approach called Continuous Descent Approach (CDA), where the landing itinerary is known to the crew well enough in advance to let the pilot descend in neutral gear without using the power of the engines until the release of the landing gear. Short-haul jets save an average of 150 kilos of kerosene with this method. SAS has applied the procedure for 2 000 landing approaches to Stockholm's Arlanda airport. SAS engineers calculated the potential savings in CO_2 emissions would have been more than 50 000 tonnes had all 108 000 landings in the past year been handled in this way. For the time being, CDA is restricted to airports with moderate traffic; improvements in air traffic control co-ordination are necessary for denser air space. Positive side-effects are improved security as the flight routes are known further ahead, and reduced noise pollution. Sweden's goal is that by 2012 three out of five planes landing in Stockholm should use the CDA method. But further measures will be needed to reach SAS' target of 20 per cent CO_2 reduction by 2020.

uses less than three litres per passenger per 100 kilometres – the figure for a small diesel-engined car. It says the plane's CO_2 emissions are as low as 80g per passenger per kilometre, half the figure for an average European car.

This figure however does not consider the non-CO_2-related climate impact of high altitude fuel combustion which is considered to result in two to four times higher impact than from carbon emissions alone (see page 120).

100 Kwh of electricity from coal
(high estimate) **105**

80 100 Kwh of electricity from coal
(low estimate)

There is further scope for saving energy in prospect with the development of alternative fuels (see page 128) and new vehicles such as **hybrid cars**.

The hybrid car is certainly one of the icons in the fight against climate change, a solution already on the market but available only to those who can afford it.

Wikipedia reads: "The hybrid vehicle, a mixture between a gasoline-powered and an electric car, typically achieves greater fuel economy and lower emissions than conventional internal combustion engine vehicles (ICEVs), resulting in fewer emissions being generated. These savings are primarily achieved by four elements of a typical hybrid design:

- *recapturing energy normally wasted during braking etc.;*
- *having significant battery storage capacity to store and reuse recaptured energy;*
- *shutting down the gasoline or diesel engine during traffic stops or while coasting or other idle periods;*
- *relying on both the gasoline (or diesel) engine and the electric motors for peak power needs, resulting in a smaller gasoline or diesel engine sized more for average usage rather than peak power usage.*

These features make a hybrid vehicle particularly efficient for city traffic where there are frequent stops, coasting and idling periods. In addition noise emissions are reduced, particularly at idling and low operating speeds, in comparison with conventional gasoline or diesel powered engine vehicles. For continuous high speed highway use these features are much less useful in reducing emissions."

The car market is moving towards more efficient and more climate-friendly vehicles, and science is experimenting with new innovative designs, for example electric cars. They might be more efficient and clean, but they impose limitations on the owner and are suitable only for short urban trips. The driving range is fairly limited (about 100 km) and the car needs re-charging for four hours.

In many countries public transport is capable of improvement, perhaps by allowing it to compete on equal terms with private operators (removing hidden subsidies, for instance) or by providing a fully integrated urban network. Some savings are possible immediately, while others will have to wait for technology to advance.

INDIVIDUALS

Making sure that every journey is necessary is one way most of us can start to reduce our emissions from travel. Earlier generations could happily talk of joy-riding, travelling for the sheer pleasure of it. The trend today is to power your joy-rides with your own energy: bicycles, roller skates, kick boards – a wide variety of vehicles are available for a nice ride in the country-side; and if you use a car, apply the principles of **eco-driving**. How many of

One of the findings of the IPCC how to tackle transport related GHG emissions was to promote improved driving practices. Results from studies conducted in Europe and the USA suggested possible improvement of 5–20% in fuel economy from eco-driving training. The mitigation costs of CO_2 by eco-driving training were mostly estimated to be negative.

Changing the way they treat their car is a step that every driver can take to improve their climate footprint. Here are some tips from the UK Government (www.direct.gov.uk/en/Environmentandgreenerliving/Greenertravel/DG_064428):

- driving smoothly can reduce fuel consumption – check the road ahead, anticipate traffic and avoid harsh acceleration and braking;
- shift to a higher gear at the right time – shift up at 2 500 rpm for petrol cars and 2 000 rpm for diesel cars. A vehicle travelling at 37 mph in third gear uses 25 per cent more fuel than it would at the same speed in fifth gear;
- get in and go – modern engines are designed to be most efficient when you do so. Keeping the engine running or pumping the accelerator wastes fuel, increases engine wear and increases emissions;
- switch your engine off if you know you will not be moving for a while;
- check your tyre pressures regularly – under-inflated tyres can increase your fuel consumption by up to 3 per cent;
- stick to the speed limits – at 110 km/h you could be using up to 30 per cent more fuel than at 80 km/h;
- remove unnecessary weight and roof racks – they increase the weight and air resistance so they increase the amount of fuel you use;
- air conditioning and other on-board electrical devices (like mobile phone chargers) increase fuel consumption, so only use them when necessary.

A lot more advice is available on the internet on how to reduce fuel consumption while driving. Other sources include:

- www.ecodrive.org;
- www.greener-driving.net (developed by UNEP);
- www.eco-drive.ch (in German);
- http://raga.ouvaton.org (in French);
- www.bedoce.com (in Spanish).

the journeys we undertake really do make us happier? When travel is really contributing to our lives, we can at any rate choose the least GHG-intensive form of transport available – preferably bike or foot, or public transport rather than private. We can also aim to be as sociable as possible when on the move. Cars with only a driver on board make very little sense, and the more **passengers** you can find the smaller each of your climate footprints

Websites where people announce where they are going and when, offering a lift to those with the same destination, have become very popular over the last few years in many places. In Germany and its neighbours the system is quite successful, and apart from providing a cheap ride between almost all medium-sized towns (for about €5 per 100 kilometre) it is a social meeting-point and a bit of an adventure for those who like it.

Some of the most popular sites are www.mitfahrgelegenheit.de (Germany, Austria, Switzerland); www.easycovoiturage.com (France); www.rideabout.com.au (Australia); www.rideshare-directory.com (United States).

will be. Set concrete goals to reduce your travel. Just as a limited calorie intake is sensible for any diet, after analysing your travelling habits and extent (see Count & Analyse) you can set a limit on how much you travel and by what means. Reducing it will have a significant effect on your costs.

CO$_2$ emissions from selected German transportation means

The results depend a lot on the occupancy rates (in pink, the average German rates used here).

Better results can be obtained for metro, tram and train if more people are using them (better network and schedules, accessibility, affordability and competitiveness compared to cars).

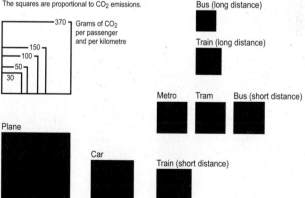

The squares are proportional to CO$_2$ emissions.

370 — Grams of CO$_2$ per passenger and per kilometre
150
100
50
30

Bus (long distance)

Train (long distance)

Metro   Tram   Bus (short distance)

Plane

Car

Train (short distance)

Source: Gunnar Gohlisch, Umweltbundesamt (German Federal Environmental Agency), 2005.

BIOFUELS

Running a car with fuel that has grown on the fields sounds like a safe and attractive option for a climate-conscious citizen. The plants grown for biofuel production absorb CO_2 from the atmosphere and combustion of the biofuel releases only the CO_2 previously absorbed by the plant. Therefore biofuels typically have far lower well-to-wheel GHG emissions than fossil fuels. With the surge in fossil fuel prices in the recent past and government programmes supporting the production of biofuels, the demand for plant-based energy has risen sharply. In the United States for example, the US Renewable Fuels Standard (RFS) required in 2006 that 1 500 million litres of the US fuel supply be provided by renewable fuels, and it is supposed to increase to 28 400 million litres in 2012.

With a further surge in demand ahead of us it is worth looking at ways to ensure a sustainable production of energy corps. Whether biofuels are "good" or "bad" is a matter of introducing a number of environmental and social safeguards.

The technical facts
Bioenergy – the use of biomass – has been and in many regions still is one of the most prominent sources of energy, in developing countries often enough inefficiently. Bioenergy refers to biomass converted to higher value and more efficient and convenient energy carriers, such as pellets, gas, or liquids. Most common liquid biofuels used for transportation are ethanol and biodiesel.

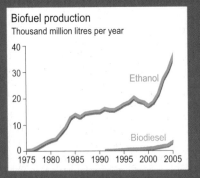

Biofuel production
Thousand million litres per year

Bioethanol is an alcohol that can be made from almost any crop that has a high content of sugar (sugarcane or sugar beet), starch crops (corn) or any cellulosic crops. The alcohol is mainly produced through a repetitive fermentation process which involves soaking, crushing or chemical extraction using a process similar to that used in

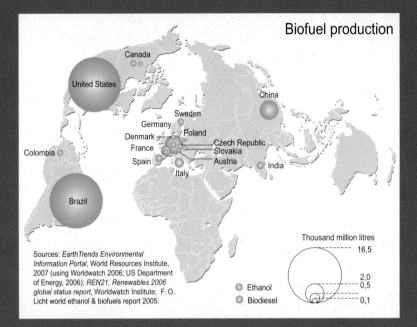

Biofuel production

Canada

United States

China

Sweden
Germany
Poland
Denmark
France
Spain
Italy
Colombia
Czech Republic
Slovakia
Austria
India

Brazil

Thousand million litres
16,5

2,0
0,5

0,1

Ethanol
Biodiesel

Sources: *EarthTrends Environmental Information Portal*, World Resources Institute, 2007 (using Worldwatch 2006; US Department of Energy, 2006); *REN21, Renewables 2006 global status report*, Worldwatch Institute; F. O. Licht world ethanol & biofuels report 2005.

beer and wine-making. Ethanol can run in an ordinary petrol car engine without modifications up to a 10 per cent blend level (some manufacturers warrant 5 per cent only, some warrant up to 15 per cent). In Brazil, where about 40 per cent of all fuel used is produced from sugar cane, all cars operate with engines slightly modified to run on blends up to 25 per cent ethanol. A car engine can be further modified (in its design and configuration) to be "flex fuel", that is to operate on fuel blends of anywhere from 0 up to 85 per cent ethanol.

Biodiesel is produced from oil, which can be sourced from oil seed crops such as rapeseed, soy bean, sunflower or jatropha and from waste oil such as cooking oil. Water and other contaminants are removed from the oil and the fatty acid content present in the oil is separated and transformed. Biodiesel can be blended with conventional diesel in vehicles, usually in a 5 per cent blend (B5).In some countries it is sold in blends up to 20 per cent (B20) or in pure form (B100) that some specially modified diesel vehicles can handle.

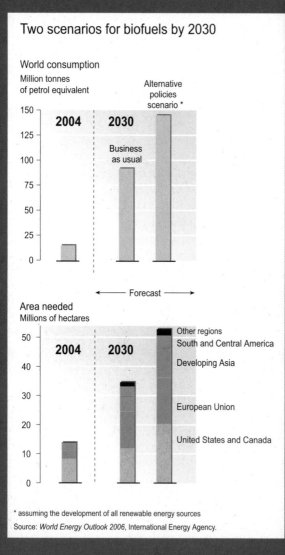

Two scenarios for biofuels by 2030

World consumption

Million tonnes
of petrol equivalent

Alternative
policies
scenario *

150 —

2004   **2030**

125 —

100 —   Business
                          as usual

75 —

50 —

25 —

0 —

←——— Forecast ———→

Area needed
Millions of hectares

50 —   ■ Other regions
                                  South and Central America
       2004   **2030**
40 —   Developing Asia

30 —

                                  European Union
20 —

10 —   United States and Canada

0 —

* assuming the development of all renewable energy sources

Source: *World Energy Outlook 2006*, International Energy Agency.

Second-generation biofuels

The technologies to produce fuels from waste from agriculture and forestry, or specific plants with high cellulose content are still a few years away from competitive commercialization. The industry assumes that second-generation biofuels will not be available in significant commercial quantities for five to 10 years. The advantages put forward are high energy efficiency, and the use of plants that grow on degraded land or in areas less important for biodiversity.

How efficient are biofuels in reducing GHGs?

In order to utilize the full potential of biofuels for reducing GHG emissions it is crucial that the total of emissions created during their production are both as low as possible and below that of their fossil alternative. There are many elements that can lead to higher greenhouse gas emissions from biofuels than in the optimal case: GHG emissions are mainly due to fossil fuel inputs into cultivation and downstream processing. But the final result also depends on the type of crops and finally the efficiency of the engine running on it. The International Energy Agency says about 15–25 per cent reduction in GHG emissions compared to fossil fuels can be achieved by using starch based crops, for example corn in the United States, but a 90 per cent reduction with sugar cane as feedstock as grown in Brasil. In some cases the climate balance of biofuels is even negative. Nitrous oxide emissions from fertilizer application during the cultivation of the plants partially reduces CO_2 emissions savings.

The controversy

Although growing fuel in fields sounds highly promising for solving our energy and climate problems, there are a number of controversial issues around biofuel production.

Energy versus Food: Sceptics are concerned that where biofuels are grown, no food will be harvested, and some even call for a moratorium. In a world where 850 million are considered undernourished any potential threat to aggravate this situation requires thorough and critical examination. Over the past three years, global food prices have risen 83 per cent. Governmental subsidies and targets for biofuel in developed countries has created a sudden increase in demand, partly responsible for the rise. Among a number of other factors are population growth and changing diets towards more energy intensive meat consumption. Energy crops may compete for land with other uses and potentially result in increased food prices. For some types of bioenergy crops marginal and waste lands are suitable. This is the case, for example, for grasses and jatropha. However, the best yields and profits arise from using good quality land, and this also applies for energy crops.

It is recognized that crop yields in much of the world are below their potential, and improved management practices could increase yields substantially, which would allow to accommodate both food and energy crops. Of the 13 200 million hectares of the world's total land area, 1 500 million hectares are used to produce arable crops and 3 500 million hectares are in pasture for meat, milk and wool production. Crops used specifically for biofuels occupy currently 25 million hectares. Many of the poor suffering from increased food prices suffer as well from increased oil prices, and local biofuel production for local use can provide substantial benefits by spurring other economic activities that would allow to raise income.

Fields versus Forests: Another threat is that the rising demand for energy crops puts pressure on forests, wetlands and other areas of high carbon stock value to win arable land, as happened in the past for soy beans or palm oil. This could cause much higher GHG emissions from released soil carbon and cleared biomass than is fixed by the cultivation of the respective crops.

Mobility versus Sustainability: Yet another concern is the way energy crops are grown. As with other intensive agricultural practices, in the absence of strictly controlled prerequisites for sustainable production, energy crop farming contributes GHG emissions from soil exploitation and the application of fertilizers. It will also increase pressure on already scarce freshwater supplies. Monocultures reduce biological diversity, decrease soil fertility and are vulnerable to pests.

Sustainability principles and criteria for biofuels
In order to make biofuels a successful tool for mitigating climate change without compromising people's livelihoods, rules for the game have to be developed. Environmental organisations, concerned countries and leading international organizations are demanding an internationally agreed certification scheme for the production of biofuels that addresses concerns related

to climate change, biodiversity, water and soil as well as labour conditions, indigenous people's rights, land rights and food security. The "UN energy report" warns: "Unless new policies are enacted to protect threatened lands, secure socially acceptable land use, and steer bioenergy development in a sustainable direction overall, the environmental and social damage could in some cases outweigh the benefits". Governments as well as the private sector need to take coordinated action to ensure sustainable production and use of biofuels, so that they may play a useful role in the transformation of the energy sector. Internationally agreed sustainability principles and criteria; identification, designation and monitoring of "no go areas" with regard to carbon storage and biodiversity potentials; social safeguards that ensure that vulnerable people are not disadvantaged through food and energy price increases, and access to modern forms of energy are among the elements taken into account by UNEP as they are collaborating with others on the development of criteria to maximize development benefits of bioenergy.

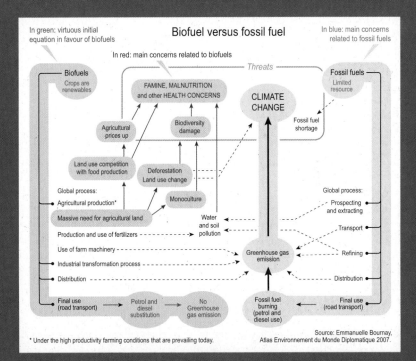

Multinationals have the opportunity to choose where to base their operations for the most profitable return. So they can decide – or not – to minimize their impact by locating production close to the point of consumption. They can also choose to ensure that their production and distribution facilities are climate-neutral. So the oil giant Shell, for example, can claim it is trying to minimize emissions from exploration, oil and gas production, shipping and refineries: "Our customers emit six to seven times more CO_2 using our products than we do making them. A small share of the energy products we make, such as electricity from our wind turbines, emit no CO_2 at all during use."

The US Pew Centre for Global Climate Change (www.pewclimate.org) reports on progress made by Deutsche Telekom, a member of its Business Environmental Leadership Council. The company's vehicle fleet's CO_2 emissions have fallen about 30 per cent from their level six years ago, thanks to the use of smaller or alternative-fuel vehicles, choosing trains instead of car or plane travel, using videoconferencing instead of travelling at all, and incorporating environmental impacts into the company's technical specifications for vehicle suppliers and manufacturers.

Corporations exert significant influence over the lives of their employees, to the extent of telling them when they have to arrive at work and leave. Staggering working hours would cut congestion and perhaps lead to an even more radical idea – telling staff to work from home. Cutting commuting would help the planet, as well as the ex-commuters' nerves.

Businesses can develop mobility plans for employees, organize car fleets, and provide incentives for using public transport for commuting to work. They can subsidize cyclists (and even simply provide proper changing and shower rooms for them at work), and buy bicycles or electrobikes. They can also draw up and apply strict rules for duty travel, requiring the use of trains for all journeys below a specified distance.

CITIES

Cities can make a significant contribution on their own account to reducing GHG emissions from transport. In fact, the same suggestions apply to cities as to businesses.

City governments can also play a key role by making low-emission transport more attractive to their citizens. Designing streets that are friendlier to pedestrians and cyclists than they are to four-wheeled vehicles will encourage more people to leave their cars at home. Integrating public transport into a seamless system which enables passengers to switch effortlessly from bus to tram or train or metro will attract more users. Some cities have introduced congestion charging systems, requiring drivers in the central area to pay a fee: they include Singapore, Stockholm, Oslo, Milan and London.

Spatial planning is an important civic function which can help significantly to cut energy use in urban transport. Cities can retain their focus and sense of place if they plan for "densification" as opposed to Los Angeles-style sprawl. By avoiding "sleeping cities" and planning mixed functions in neighbourhoods, commuting can be minimized. This can save GHG emissions, because energy consumption in cities is directly linked to the number of inhabitants per square kilometre.

Abu Dhabi, in the United Arab Emirates, is planning a new city, to be called Masdar, which will rely entirely on solar energy, with a sustainable, zero-carbon, zero-waste ecology. It will cover six square kilometres and house energy, science and technology communities. Masdar has been planned as a high-density city, with electric-powered vehicles providing public transport. The designers, the British architectural firm Foster and Partners, say: "Rooted in a zero carbon ambition, the city itself is car-free. With a maximum distance of 200 metres to the nearest transport link and amenities, the compact network of streets encourages walking and is complemented by a personalized rapid transport system. The shaded walkways and narrow streets will create a pedestrian-friendly environment in the context of Abu Dhabi's extreme climate. It also articulates the tightly planned, compact nature of traditional walled cities."

A Chinese city, Dongtan, hopes to be the world's first sustainable city, with all the buildings powered by renewable energy, and self-sufficient in water

Transport-related energy consumption
Gigajoules per capita per year

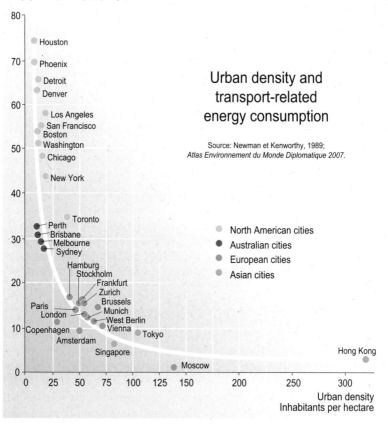

Urban density and transport-related energy consumption

Source: Newman et Kenworthy, 1989;
Atlas Environnement du Monde Diplomatique 2007.

○ North American cities
● Australian cities
○ European cities
○ Asian cities

and food from the surrounding farmland. The first phase of the city will house up to 80 000 people by 2020 and citizens will be encouraged to make use of the zero-carbon public transport, which will be powered entirely by renewable energy. People arriving at Dongtan, near Shanghai, will leave their cars outside the city, travelling along the shore on foot, bicycle or sustainable public transport. The only vehicles allowed in the city will be powered by electricity or hydrogen. Dongtan will produce its own energy from wind, solar, biofuels and recycled city waste. Gas will be made from rice husks, a by-product of nearby rice mills. A network of cycle and foot paths will help the city achieve **close to zero vehicle emissions**. Farmland

More and more cities are trying to address the invasion by cars of city centres by charging a fee to discourage drivers from using their private vehicles. Together with a reduction of nuisance and health hazards such as noise and air pollution, the fee can reduce CO_2 emissions considerably. London's congestion charge resulted in a decrease of 16.4 per cent of CO_2 emissions in the city because of traffic reduction and a better traffic flow in the first year after its introduction in 2003. Today, compared with 2002, traffic entering the zone is down by 21 per cent, and cycling has increased by 43 per cent.

More recent examples of cities that have introduced congestion charges on a trial basis are Stockholm and Milan. Considered one of Europe's ten most polluted cities, Milan introduced an "anti-smog" ticket called the eco-pass at the start of 2008, to reduce air pollution in the city centre. This will run for a one-year trial period.

The fee charged is based on the vehicle engine type, and particularly addresses older petrol and diesel vehicles. The eco-pass does not apply to mopeds, motorbikes, or alternative-fuel vehicles (e.g. hybrid or electrical cars). It costs €2-10 to drive in the city centre, an area of about 8 square kilometres. Cameras at 43 electric gates monitor traffic and violators face fines starting at €70. The city council expects to generate €24 million, which will be used for buying buses and green vehicles, and for creating bicycle paths.

The first month produced excellent results, with pollution levels dropping, traffic reduced by 22.7 per cent, and 9.1 per cent more people using subway trains to reach the city centre. The highest reduction in car usage came from the most polluting cars which faced higher prices to enter the zone: their number dropped by 40 per cent.

within the Dongtan site will use organic methods.

The Stockholm Environment Institute (SEI) describes the global environmental imbalance as: "Sustainability requires living within the regenerative capacity of the planet. Currently, human demand on the planet is exceeding its regenerative capacity by about 20 per cent. This is called *overshoot.*" Dongtan's architects are developing an ideal ecological footprint for the city to guide the master plan and prevent overshoot. Its footprint will be determined by a modelling programme called the Resources and Energy Analysis Programme (REAP), developed by SEI and the Centre for Urban and Regional Ecology at the University of Manchester, UK. Unlike the traditional focus on air and water pollution, REAP concentrates on measuring the amount of resources consumed by the number of individuals occupying a defined area. This will inevitably include the consumption of fossil fuels.

CITIES

Inspired by similar schemes in Curitiba and Bogota, Jakarta built a 12.9 kilometre rapid transport system in nine months. There are now six further routes, and plans for more, all using diesel and compressed natural gas buses. The network saves an estimated 120 000 tonnes of CO_2 a year, and has improved safety and efficiency.

Mexico City has replaced 3 000 taxis with more fuel-efficient models. The municipal government, with support from a local bank, is providing 15 000 pesos (approximately US$1 375) to each driver wishing to replace his old taxi with a new vehicle, costing about 70 000 pesos (US$6 420). The remaining sum is repaid via a bank loan over about four years, with drivers paying 760 to 870 pesos a month (about US$70–80). The city's 103 000 taxis account for 35 per cent of transport emissions. The programme aims to replace 10 000 old taxis by 2012. The project shows how vital it is to work in partnership with other parts of government, including the environment and transport ministries.

Seoul is trying – with some success – to show its people that there are other ways of getting round the city apart from the car. Its Weekly No Driving Day programme is improving air quality, cutting congestion and saving energy. Every year, 2 million cars stay off the road, reducing CO_2 vehicle emissions by 10 per cent – a total of 2 million tonnes of CO_2. The improved air quality is improving residents' health, saving the city millions annually. The programme – which is voluntary – works because it is applied on weekdays, which encourages people to find other ways to and from work. Participants are given incentives, like discounted petrol, free parking and car washing, to use alternate modes of transport on their chosen day. They are encouraged to take part as often as they can. Those participating just three times a year, for example, will have their incentives removed or reduced.

Cycling can be made attractive even in chilly northern Europe. In the Danish capital, Copenhagen, "the City of Cyclists", more than 36 per cent of the population cycles to work every day, and the city saves about 90 000 tonnes of CO_2 emissions annually. Bikes are as fast as cars and buses over distances of up to five kilometres. Despite a dramatic growth in their use during the last ten years, the number of accidents has fallen substantially. There are

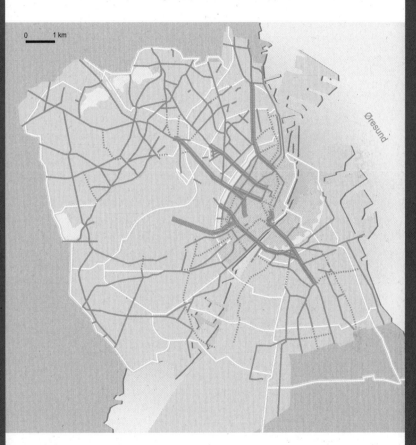

Copenhagen, paradise for cyclists

0   1 km

Øresund

——— Existing cycle track

.... Cycle track under development or planned

≈≈≈ "Green route" for longer cycle journeys

▨▨▨ Route used by more than 10 000 cycles and mopeds a day

▨ Central area where the city council provides free cycles

In Copenhagen 36 per cent of the city's inhabitants cycle to work, using a network of more than 330 kilometres of cycle tracks and travelling at an average speed of 15 kph.

Sources: *Cycle Policy 2002-2012*; *Bicycle account 2004*, City of Copenhagen.

over 120 racks throughout central Copenhagen where bikes can be obtained by inserting a DKK20 coin (about US$3) into the bicycle's lock as a deposit. After use the bike can be returned to any of the racks and the coin will be returned automatically. Infrastructure includes cycle lanes, dedicated cycle tracks on either side of all main roads, and some bike parks at railway stations and bus terminals. Bikes are allowed on many trains, and on the metro outside peak hours.

All emissions from extraction to combustion of one tonne of petrol

3 760

The scope for countries to move their people onto sustainable, climate-friendly travel paths is massive. They can enforce road speed limits, provide good public transport nationwide, ensure adequate production of biofuels, or require planners to design cities around walkers and cyclists, avoiding urban sprawl and its consequences of long commuting distances, and encourage mixed neighbourhoods of activity and housing. They can ensure that private transport pays its true share of the costs of infrastructure by increasing road and petrol taxes. They can act together to see that international travel (mainly by air and sea) bears the environmental costs of its activities, for instance by demanding that aviation fuel is taxed in a way that gives no country an advantage over others.

The Netherlands, Portugal, and Finland charge different rates for car registration to encourage buyers to choose the cleanest models. The Dutch version means the new registration taxes, payable when a car is sold to its first buyer, can earn the owner of a hybrid a discount up to €6 000 (US$9 400). Austria has had a registration tax based on fuel consumption for several years.

Shelter

Worldwide energy consumption is projected to increase by 54 per cent from 2001 levels by 2025. The UK's Energy Saving Trust says over a quarter of all the country's CO_2 emissions come from individual homes, with the average household producing six tonnes of CO_2 every year. But £7.5 thousand million (US$14.85 thousand million) worth of the energy used every year in British households is wasted. Of the electricity used in the UK, £3 thousand million (US$5.9 thousand million) worth annually goes on powering consumer electronic and computer products – 30 per cent of the average household electricity bill.

There are devices which will let you see how much energy your home is using. So-called "smart meters" available for less than US$100 monitor electricity supply while providing real-time monetary information about the household's energy use. When lights and appliances are turned on, the bat-

Combustion of one tonne of crude oil

3 060

36 Running a 100 watt bulb for 20 days

tery-powered device reveals exactly how much electricity is being *used*, how

Studies have shown that a single family can easily consume twice as much as their next-door neighbours. When people in charge of their homes know their electricity use is being monitored, if falls dramatically. In another study, where people were given the chance of comparing their energy consumption with the same month in the previous year or with their neighbours, the upshot was an energy saving of 5 per cent. So keeping track of our energy consumption will very likely make us switch off the lights when we leave the kitchen.

the cost of electricity per hour changes, and how much CO_2 the household is producing. In the UK for example, each £100 (US$201) of electricity saved at home means 500 kg of CO_2 avoided at the power station, and almost a quarter of a tonne of fossil fuel saved.

ENERGY ALTERNATIVES

Even if we use the enormous potential for saving energy unnecessarily spent, we need to intensify in parallel the development of energy production technologies as an alternative to fossil energy. The generation of nuclear energy does not emit CO_2 in the energy generation process (but during uranium mining, transport and waste storage). It has therefore gained many advocates recently in the debate around CO_2 reductions and responses to growing energy demands. Nuclear energy is based on uranium as raw material input. Uranium reserves are estimated to last no longer than oil, and thus nuclear energy can only offer an intermediate solution as an alternative energy provider. Nuclear energy supporters downplay the enormous risks associated to an operating nuclear power plant. But because of those and the unresolved problem of storing increasing amounts of radioactive wastes resulting from nuclear fission, the development of new nuclear powerplants is in many countries all but well accepted among citizens.

The International Energy Agency, keen to promote the use of the most abundant energy source of all, the sun, has started a Solar Heating and Cooling Programme (www.iea-shc.org/solarenergy). Solar thermal energy is appropriate for both uses. Key applications for solar technologies are those that require low temperature heat, such as domestic water heating, space heating, pool heating, drying processes, and some industrial processes. Solar cooling works where the supply of sunny summer days is well matched with the demand – the desire for coolness indoors. The Agency says the main barriers preventing the greater use of solar energy are cost, the way current government policies benefit non-solar technologies, and the failure to take into account the environmental costs of using fossil fuels. Its programme is working to educate users and decision makers, expand the solar thermal market, and carry out research, development and testing of hardware, materials and designs.

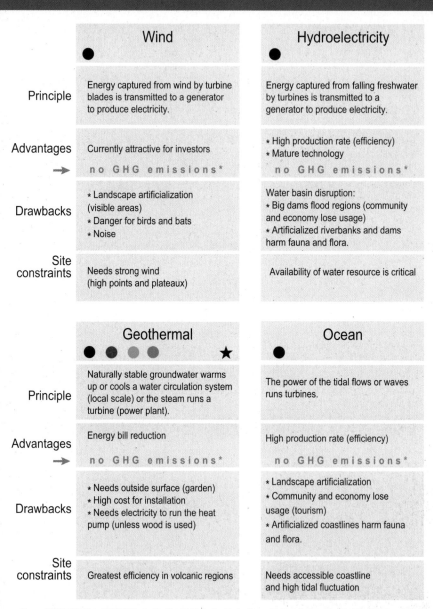

	Wind	**Hydroelectricity**
Principle	Energy captured from wind by turbine blades is transmitted to a generator to produce electricity.	Energy captured from falling freshwater by turbines is transmitted to a generator to produce electricity.
Advantages →	Currently attractive for investors no GHG emissions*	* High production rate (efficiency) * Mature technology no GHG emissions*
Drawbacks	* Landscape artificialization (visible areas) * Danger for birds and bats * Noise	Water basin disruption: * Big dams flood regions (community and economy lose usage) * Artificialized riverbanks and dams harm fauna and flora.
Site constraints	Needs strong wind (high points and plateaux)	Availability of water resource is critical

	Geothermal ★	**Ocean**
Principle	Naturally stable groundwater warms up or cools a water circulation system (local scale) or the steam runs a turbine (power plant).	The power of the tidal flows or waves runs turbines.
Advantages →	Energy bill reduction no GHG emissions*	High production rate (efficiency) no GHG emissions*
Drawbacks	* Needs outside surface (garden) * High cost for installation * Needs electricity to run the heat pump (unless wood is used)	* Landscape artificialization * Community and economy lose usage (tourism) * Artificialized coastlines harm fauna and flora.
Site constraints	Greatest efficiency in volcanic regions	Needs accessible coastline and high tidal fluctuation

Source: UNEP-GRID-Arendal, *Vital Climate Graphics*, 2005; Godfrey Boyle, *Renewable Energy: Power for a Sustainable Future*, 2004.

Solar (photovoltaic)

A semiconductor cell (usually made from silicon) converts sunlight directly into electricity.

Currently attractive for investors
Minimal maintenance
no GHG emissions*

* Needs large panel surface
* Used cells are hazardous waste
* Visual impact

Depends on length of daily sunlight and intensity

Solar thermal

A surface absorbs and transfers heat and light radiated from the sun to a fluid.

Energy bill reduction
Minimal maintenance
no GHG emissions*

* Needs large panel surface
* Used cells are hazardous waste
* Visual impact

Depends on length of daily sunlight and intensity

Introducing the main **renewable** energies

Applications:
● Electricity production
● Industrial process
● Heating or cooling buildings
● Warming water
● Transport

★ On-site use mostly

Biomass

Wood

The steam from wood burning runs a turbine or is used directly for the building.

Feedstock can be wastewood

Problematic at industrial scale (planting fast-growing trees, monoculture)

GHG emissions from land use change

Distance to wood production areas is critical

Waste

Methane from waste decomposition is harnessed to produce heat or run a turbine.

* Uses waste as a resource
* Reduces methane emissions
no GHG emissions*

Biogas needs to be "cleaned" of corrosive hydrogen sulfide

Distance to landfill / manure production areas is critical

Biofuels
(ethanol and biodiesel)

Either alcohol (from sugar, starch or cellulose crops fermentation) or oil is used to fuel engines.

Replace fossil fuel burning from transport

Problematic at industrial scale:
* Surface competition with food crops, monoculture
* Deforestation, fertilizers
GHG emissions from land use change ←

Availability of agricultural lands is critical

* If you except indirect emissions from building the plants, dams, turbines, solar panels, etc.

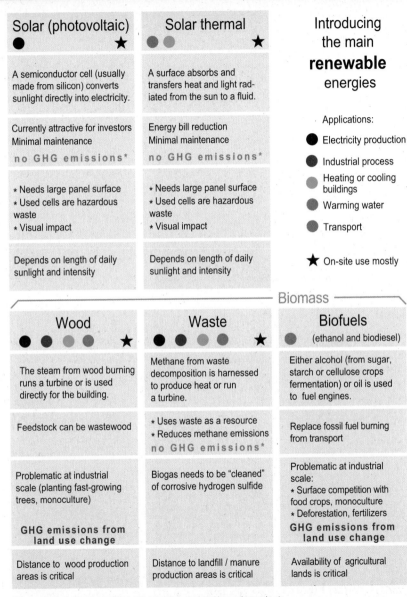

Even though the nuclear industry does not significantly contribute to greenhouse gas emissions, it is a disputable alternative to fossil fuels. In the former USSR people and the environment still have to cope with the nuclear industry's legacy.

Kola

Greifswald
Baltic Sea
ESTONIA
Saint-Petersburg
Leningradskaïa NPS
(Sosnovy Bor)
EX-RDA
Wismut
LATVIA
Kalininskaïa NPS
(Tver)
RUSSIA
Ignalina
CZECH
REPUBLIC
POLAND
LITHUANIA
Temelin
BELARUS
Minsk
Smolenskaïa NPS
Moscow
Nijni Novgorod
Dukovany
Highly contaminated zone:
forbidden or controlled access
Kazan
Bohunice
Mochovce
Rovenskaïa NPS
Chernobyl
Sarov
(Arzamas-16)
SLOVENIE
Krsko
SLOVAKIA
CROATIA
HUNGARY
Khmelnitskaïa NPS
Kourskaïa NPS
Samara
Paks-Tolna
Kiev
Novovoronejskaïa NPS
BOSNIA-
HERZEGOVINA
UKRAINE
Zarechnyy
(Penza-19)
Balakovo
SERBIA
ROUMANIA
MOLDOVA
RUSSIA
MONTENEGRO
Zaporojskaïa NPS
KOSOVO
Kozloduy
Ioujnoukrainskaïa NPS
Kapustin
Yar
ALBANIA
Danube
Volgograd
MACEDONIA
Belene
Cernavoda
Azgyr
BULGARIA
Volgodonsk
Black Sea
Astrakhan

Aktau

Source: Philippe Rekacewicz, *Atlas Environnement du Monde Diplomatique 2007*, using the following as primary sources.

Field reporting: Philippe Rekacewicz and Ieva Rucevska, 2002, 2003 and 2004; ENVSEC Environment and Security Initiative; Michael Glantz et al., *Water, Climate, and Development Issues in the Amudarya Basin*, Informal Planning Meeting, June 2002; The Franklin Institute, Philadelphie, Pennsylvania; *Addressing Environmental Risks in Central Asia, Risks, Conditions, Policies, Capacities*, UNDP, Bratislava, 2003; United Nations Children's Fund, TransMONEE database (www.unicef-irc.org/databases/transmonee); *The Road to Stability and Prosperity in South Eastern Europe*, Regional Strategy Paper, World Bank, 2000; *Europe and Central Asia Region, Transition - The First Ten Years: Analysis and Lessons for Eastern Europe and the former Soviet Union*, World Bank, 2002; Kenley Butler, *Weapons of Mass Destruction in Central Asia*, Nuclear Threat Initiative, 2002.

GEORGIA
Metsamor
AZERBAIJAN
ARMENIA
Baku
Caspian
Sea

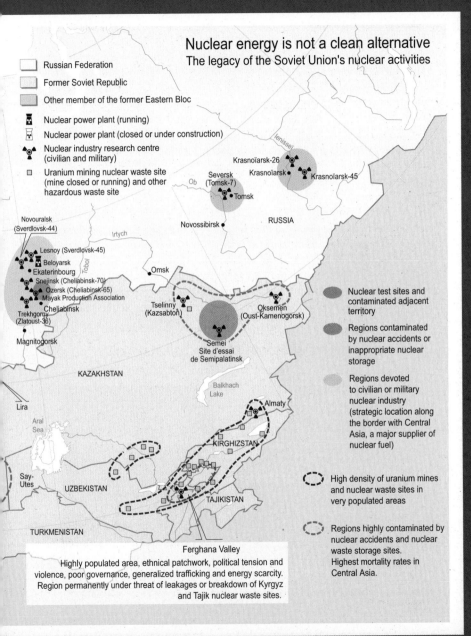

Nuclear energy is not a clean alternative
The legacy of the Soviet Union's nuclear activities

Russian Federation

Former Soviet Republic

Other member of the former Eastern Bloc

Nuclear power plant (running)

Nuclear power plant (closed or under construction)

Nuclear industry research centre (civilian and military)

Uranium mining nuclear waste site (mine closed or running) and other hazardous waste site

Nuclear test sites and contaminated adjacent territory

Regions contaminated by nuclear accidents or inappropriate nuclear storage

Regions devoted to civilian or military nuclear industry (strategic location along the border with Central Asia, a major supplier of nuclear fuel)

High density of uranium mines and nuclear waste sites in very populated areas

Regions highly contaminated by nuclear accidents and nuclear waste storage sites. Highest mortality rates in Central Asia.

Krasnoïarsk-26

Krasnoïarsk

Krasnoïarsk-45

Seversk (Tomsk-7)

Ienisseï

Ob

• Tomsk

RUSSIA

Novossibirsk •

Novouralsk (Sverdlovsk-44)

Irtych

▲ Lesnoy (Sverdlovsk-45)

Beloyarsk

Ekaterinbourg

Snejinsk (Cheliabinsk-70)

Ozersk (Cheliabinsk-65)

Mayak Production Association

Cheliabinsk

Trekhgorny (Zlatoust-36)

Magnitogorsk

Tobol

• Omsk

Tselinny (Kazsabton)

Oksemen (Oust-Kamenogorsk)

Semeï Site d'essai de Semipalatinsk

KAZAKHSTAN

Balkhach Lake

Lira

Aral Sea

Almaty

KIRGHIZSTAN

Say-Utes

UZBEKISTAN

TAJIKISTAN

TURKMENISTAN

Ferghana Valley

Highly populated area, ethnical patchwork, political tension and violence, poor governance, generalized trafficking and energy scarcity. Region permanently under threat of leakages or breakdown of Kyrgyz and Tajik nuclear waste sites.

It makes sense to try to get your house to do most of the work for you without needing much energy at all. That may sound too good to be true, but it is not. Germany has done a lot of work on the idea of the Passive House, one which relies on its own intrinsic design as far as possible to meet its energy requirements (www.passiv.de). A house of this sort will have good insulation, will face south, and have the best level of glazing available. It will be airtight, will pre-heat fresh air with a ground heat-exchanger and recover waste heat from air leaving the building, and will use renewable energy to heat the water.

Perhaps a house like this is not an option for you, let alone one which keeps itself warm in winter and cools in summer as well, like the ancient wind towers of Yemen and other parts of the Middle East which are designed to make maximum use of natural ventilation. But you do always have the option of remembering how much energy went into building your house, how much it needs to keep it going in the style you have adopted, and what the scope is for saving energy – from not overfilling your kettle, to using

Energy cost of various construction materials

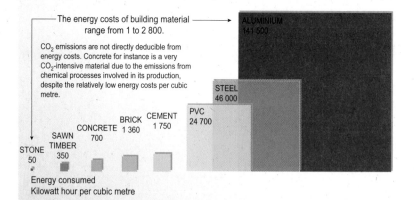

The energy costs of building material range from 1 to 2 800.

CO_2 emissions are not directly deducible from energy costs. Concrete for instance is a very CO_2-intensive material due to the emissions from chemical processes involved in its production, despite the relatively low energy costs per cubic metre.

ALUMINIUM 141 500

STEEL 46 000

PVC 24 700

CEMENT 1 750

BRICK 1 360

CONCRETE 700

SAWN TIMBER 350

STONE 50

Energy consumed
Kilowatt hour per cubic metre

Sources: *Atlas Environnement du Monde Diplomatique, 2007;* Federation of Natural Stone Industries (SN Roc); CTBA, *L'Essentiel sur le bois, 2001.*

Eco-design strategies

Super insulation	High efficiency insulation materials, often including gases with extremely low heat transfer values
High-performance windows	Windows combining high level of light penetration with low level of heat transfer, for example double-glazed windows.
Ventilation heat recovery systems	Ventilation system that uses outgoing heated indoor air to pre-heat incoming cold air.
Ground couple heat exchangers	Uses the more stable ground temperature (cooler on hot days and warmer of cold days) to adjust the temperature of incoming air.
Sunspaces	Spaces heated by direct sun light.
Materials with high thermal storage capacities	Materials that keep their temperature for extended periods of time, even if the surrounding air temperature changes, hence storing heat gained during a hot day to heat the building during a cold night, and vice versa.
Active solar water systems	Water heating through direct sunlight, for example by leading water through pipes located in the centre of concave steel mirrors focussing sun light on the pipes.
Photovoltaic systems	Panels with semi-conductor cells convert sun light to electricity
Integrated mechanical system	Automated features of a building, e.g. sunshades, responding to incoming sun light or indoor temperature so as to maintain confortable conditions.
Home automation systems	Computer controlled heating, cooling and ventilation adjusting the indoor temperature and ventilation according to pre-set parameters, often designed to minimize energy use.
Energy-efficient lights and appliances	Appliances and lights meeting minimum criteria for energy use per output. For example, low-energy lamps often use about 30-40% less energy to provide the same levels of light as ordinary lamps do.

Source: IEA task 13 low energy buildings (1989-1993)) cited in United Nations Environment Programme (UNEP), Buildings and Climate Change, Status, Challenges and Opportunities, 2007.

Energy consumption and CO$_2$ emissions from building

Energy consumption for heating and hot water
Kilowatt hour per square metre per year

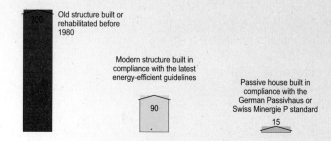

Old structure built or rehabilitated before 1980

300

Modern structure built in compliance with the latest energy-efficient guidelines

90

Passive house built in compliance with the German Passivhaus or Swiss Minergie P standard

15

CO$_2$ emissions depending on the energy used for heating and hot water, for a 100 square metre dwelling

Kilograms of carbon equivalent per year

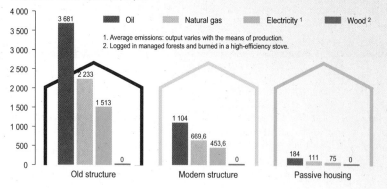

■ Oil   Natural gas   Electricity[1]   Wood[2]

1. Average emissions: output varies with the means of production.
2. Logged in managed forests and burned in a high-efficiency stove.

Old structure: 3 681, 2 233, 1 513, 0
Modern structure: 1 104, 669,6, 453,6, 0
Passive housing: 184, 111, 75, 0

Sources: Cécile Marin, *Atlas Environnement du Monde Diplomatique, 2007;* La Maison écologique, n° 37, February-March 2007; Effinergie; Minergie; Passivhaus; Ademe.

energy-efficient **light bulbs** and turning appliances off (and unplugging

Fifty per cent of emissions related to lighting in a house can be reduced by replacing old incandescent lights with the lowest energy versions available. Optimized design to make the best use of daylight cuts the remaining 50 per cent in half again.

Those who have no access to any form of modern energy, about a third of the world's people, burn fossil fuels directly, representing about 1 per cent of the world's lighting and about 20 per cent of lighting-related GHG emissions. This is just one example of how money and knowledge could very well be invested to improve people's living situations and create a positive impact for the whole world.

them) when you do not need them. There is a lot you can do in your house without having to rebuild it or invest a lot of money, and most activities that cut your energy consumption will also reduce your energy bill.

SMALL AND LARGE ORGANIZATIONS

Energy efficient lighting (lighting can account for up to 40 per cent of a company's total electricity bill) makes sense. Simpler still, make use where you can of sunlight and natural shade. Make sure heating and cooling are provided where they are needed and nowhere else. Save water – mend that dripping tap. Save it out of doors as well, by mulching a garden, using timed irrigation or irrigating at night. Reuse water, collect the rain that pours off the roof – it is free and requires not much effort to use it for simple purposes. Guidelines and organizations that provide businesses with useful information on how reduction can be achieved and how it works for business exist. One of them is the is the study by the World Business Council for Sustainable Development (WBCSD), *Energy Efficiency in Buildings: Business Realities and Opportunities*, which promotes the idea of zero net energy buildings.

Computers and other IT installations are remarkable energy consumers. The Wuppertal Institute for Climate, Environment and Energy calculates that the production of one PC requires 3 000 kWh (that is about as much as a family consumes in a year) and 1.5 tonnes of raw materials. Data centres (also called server farms) are where companies like Google or Amazon or internet service providers locate the hundreds or thousands of computer servers that provide their online services. Data centres use massive amounts of electricity; large ones can use megawatts of power, with each square meter using as much power as an entire average US home. Cooling is about 60 per cent of the power costs in a data centre because of inefficiency. The IT industry has realised the need for action which at the same time is of course a business opportunity for many. It has responded by developing more efficient and therefore more environmentally friendly products, known as "Green Computing" or **"Green IT"**.

The work habits of computer users and businesses can be modified to minimize environmental damage. Here are some steps you can take:
- *power down the CPU and all peripherals during extended periods of inactivity;*
- *try to do computer-related tasks during continuous, intensive blocks of time, leaving hardware off at other times;*
- *power up and power down energy-intensive peripherals such as laser printers only when you need them;*
- *use liquid crystal display (LCD) rather than cathode-ray-tube (CRT) monitors;*
- *use notebooks rather than desktop computers whenever possible;*
- *use the power-management features to turn off hard drives and displays after several minutes of inactivity;*
- *minimize the use of paper, and properly recycle waste paper;*
- *dispose of e-waste properly;*
- *use alternative energy sources for computing workstations, servers, networks and data centres.*

Best Practices for Data Centres – Lessons Learned from Benchmarking 22 Data Centres: http://eetd.lbl.gov/emills/PUBS/PDF/ACEEE-datacenters.pdf.

Greening The Data Centre – A Five-Step Method for CIOs and Data Center Managers: http://greenit.net/downloads/GreenIT-Greening-Data-Center-5-Step-Process.pdf.

IBM for example in May 2007 launched its "Project Big Green" in which the company is redirecting US$1 thousand million per year across its businesses, mobilising its resources to dramatically increase the level of energy efficiency in IT. The plan includes new products and services for IBM and its clients to sharply reduce data centre energy consumption, transforming the business and public technology infrastructures into "green" data centres.

The company reports that the savings are substantial – for an average 25 000 square foot data centre, clients should be able to achieve 42 per cent energy savings. Based on the energy mix in the US, this saving equates to 7 439 tonnes of carbon emissions saved per year.

In their governance role cities can be careful to get their own house in order, greening every aspect of the administration. When renovating public buildings, for example, insulation should always be completed to high energy-efficiency standards. Renewable energy should be sought for heating systems (about 70 per cent of London's CO_2 emissions come from powering the city's buildings, domestic, commercial and public). The maintenance of parks can help to achieve GHG emission reductions, for instance through minimal fertilizer use and the planting of low-maintenance plant species. London hopes to become the world's first city to use light-emitting diodes (LED) for all its street lighting by 2013. LED lighting uses up to 40 per cent less energy than conventional street lights, while providing improved vision. Geneva's new public lighting scheme expects to reduce CO_2 emissions just by replacing inefficient street lamps with ones which will give better light. An investment of around €3 million is expected to save 21–30 per cent of the electricity used, and a corresponding percentage of CO_2.

The Climate Alliance of European Cities with Indigenous Rainforest Peoples (www.klimabuendnis.org/start.htm) works with local authorities to reduce their GHG emissions. It says an obvious starting point is their own energy consumption, which represents between 3 and 10 per cent of total energy use in a city or municipality. This includes heat and electricity used in municipal offices or for street lighting, sewage treatment, water pumping, municipal car fleets, swimming pools, etc. Schools and housing may also be a municipal responsibility. Many local authorities have reduced their energy demand by up to 15 per cent, without major investment, simply through energy management techniques like monitoring consumption, improving control, and early recognition and elimination of weak points. Steps that involve building users can be highly successful, for example awareness-raising and motivation, and sometimes cities offer incentives by sharing the savings with building users.

Local authorities can systematically plan for energy efficiency by retrofitting buildings and heating systems, installing efficient lighting systems, and building combined heat and power units in large public buildings. They can also have a considerable influence on energy demand in the private sector. Many municipal energy utilities apply demand-side policies, offering advice and incentives for efficient devices and integrated energy services in the heating sector.

Lighting a house for a year
(rich countries)

135

(5,5) Producing 100 Kwh of photovoltaic electricity at mid-latitudes

Some are encouraging the establishment of ecological housing developments, where leases are granted with specific conditions attached about how the beneficiary should build and run their building. London plans to use this approach and it is already a reality in the south of the city at the **BedZED** development (www.peabody.org.uk/pages/GetPage.aspx?id=179).

"Eco-neighbourhoods" usually build on a holistic concept of sustainability, including minimal energy consumption and waste generation principles of social mixing and economic solidarity. At BedZED (the Beddington Zero Energy Development), only energy from renewable sources is used to meet the needs of the development, so it adds no CO2 to the atmosphere. BedZED provides 82 residential homes, and the project also includes buildings for commercial use, an exhibition centre, and a children's nursery. Buildings are constructed from thermally massive materials that store heat during warm conditions and release it at cooler times. In addition, all buildings are enclosed in a 30 centimetre insulation jacket. The houses are arranged in south-facing terraces to maximize heat gain from the sun, an approach known as passive solar gain. Each terrace is backed by north-facing offices, where minimal solar gain reduces the tendency to overheat and the need for energy-hungry air conditioning. Heat from the sun and that generated by occupants and everyday activities such as cooking is sufficient to heat homes to a comfortable temperature. The need for space heating is therefore reduced or completely eliminated.

Other well-known examples of sustainable neighbourhoods are Vauban in Freiburg (southern Germany), and Bo1 in Malmö (Sweden). You can find a list of American eco-neighbourhoods at www.treehugger.com/files/2008/01/americas_10_bes.php.

Cities are sometimes able to subsidize zero-energy buildings, private initiatives for solar and photovoltaic panels and geothermal heating. They can also encourage the renovation of private housing stock for rental by providing subsidies for improvements that help to save a defined percentage of energy.

Energy consumption by usage in a building

Buildings (residential and commercial) account for 10 to 15% of all greenhouse gas emissions, including almost 70% carbon dioxide and 25% methane.

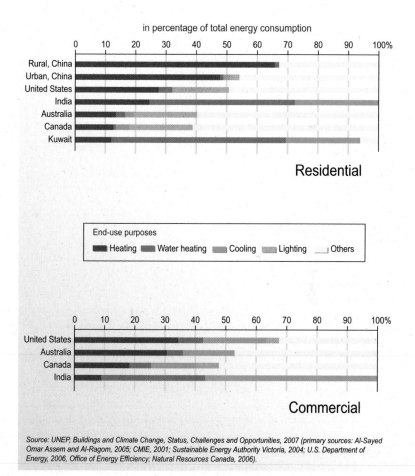

in percentage of total energy consumption

Rural, China
Urban, China
United States
India
Australia
Canada
Kuwait

Residential

End-use purposes

Heating Water heating Cooling Lighting Others

United States
Australia
Canada
India

Commercial

Source: UNEP, Buildings and Climate Change, Status, Challenges and Opportunities, 2007 (primary sources: Al-Sayed Omar Assem and Al-Ragom, 2005; CMIE, 2001; Sustainable Energy Authority Victoria, 2004; U.S. Department of Energy, 2006, Office of Energy Efficiency; Natural Resources Canada, 2006).

Greenhouse gas intensity of national economies

The national greenhouse gas intensity measures the quantity of GHG emissions in relation to the economic output of a country and is independent of the absolute quantity of GHG emitted. Other ways to represent GHG emissions are emissions per capita or in total per country. In both cases the picture changes completely. Countries with high absolute emissions may have relatively low intensities and vice versa, as with growing economic productivity efficiency tends to increase, and economic activities shift from industrial to the service sector. On the other hand, countries with high intensity may well have very low per capita emissions. See pages 22 and 48 for alternative rankings of emitters.

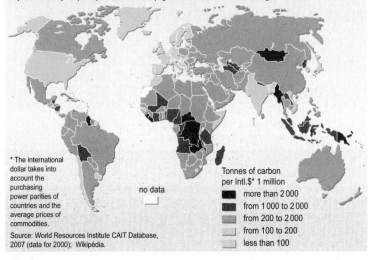

* The international dollar takes into account the purchasing power parities of countries and the average prices of commodities.

no data

Source: World Resources Institute CAIT Database, 2007 (data for 2000); Wikipédia.

Tonnes of carbon per Intl.$* 1 million
- more than 2 000
- from 1 000 to 2 000
- from 200 to 2 000
- from 100 to 200
- less than 100

COUNTRIES

As with everyone else, the bottom line for countries is to save money, and one way of doing that is by saving energy. An example is China, which has announced that it will invest 1.5 trillion yuan (US$193 thousand million) by making existing buildings more energy efficient by 2020 so as to save millions of tonnes of coal. Warning that wasted energy was slowing economic growth, the Vice-Minister of Construction, Qiu Baoxing, said 350 million tonnes of coal could be saved in 15 years if existing buildings were renovated to make them more efficient, and if new buildings met green standards.

From 1980 to 2006 China's energy consumption increased by 5.6 per cent annually, boosting the 9.8 per cent annual growth in its economy. But energy consumption for every 10 000 yuan of GDP dropped from 3.39 tonnes of standard coal in 1980 to 1.21 tonnes in 2006, an annual energy-saving rate 3.9 per cent.

Act: Offset

Whether one is fat or thin, part of the rich in the developed or of the poor in the developing world, or the other way around, what counts is the obvious fact that there is only one atmosphere. Therefore, the argument runs, greenhouse gas emissions saved by one person or in one country are just as valuable as savings by someone else: the atmosphere will still benefit. So if someone wants to emit more than they want to or are allowed to, why not simply pay to help reducing emissions elsewhere? If you want to make a trans-Atlantic flight, for example, then counteract the climate damage you are doing by paying for a specific number of **trees** to be planted to soak up

One mystery that puzzles many people considering offsets is working out how much carbon reduction they will really achieve, particularly for projects which sequester carbon. And a question often asked about forestry projects is how permanent their effects will be. For example, during the life-cycle of a tree it will absorb a certain amount of carbon. But if it is burnt or rots away, some of this stored carbon will be released into the atmosphere again. New trees planted will always absorb CO_2 as they grow, but if the land was cleared of a natural forest, or another carbon sink, the net effect may be much lower, or even negative. There is also scientific debate over the usefulness of tree planting as a remedy for climate change anyway, with evidence that it may well work at lower latitudes but in temperate regions may even have a warming effect, because the tree canopy absorbs sunlight rather than reflecting it.

There can be other problems with tree-based offsets too. Restoring natural forests may be good. But creating plantations of a single species will produce few benefits for people or wildlife. Non-native fast-growing (and commercially attractive) species like thirsty eucalyptus can cause havoc to local ecosystems.

But trees still have a lot to offer. For a start they are a cheap way of removing CO_2 from the atmosphere: US$90 will pay for 900 trees, enough to remove as much carbon annually as the average American generates each year from fossil fuels. They can be a source of fuel wood and therefore slow deforestation. They also help wildlife to thrive, slow down soil erosion, provide timber, fruit and other products – and they are potent symbols of environmental health which most of us recognize. But each time a tree is lost it should be replaced. In short, planting a tree is almost always a good thing. Not all trees planted, however, can be considered as offsets.

the carbon you generate. This is the system known as **carbon offsetting**.

To put it simply, carbon offsets aim to neutralize the amount of your GHG contribution by taking your money to fund projects which should cause an equal reduction of emissions somewhere, some day. Greenhouse gases circulate freely in the one atmosphere we all share, so compensating our own emissions can be achieved anywhere in the world. In order to make this quite straightforward idea work, it is important that the emission reduction would not have taken place without the extra incentive provided by emission reduction credits – in other words, we should not be able to claim the credits for something that would have happened anyway.

Offsetting GHG emissions, the act of compensating for your emissions elsewhere, builds on the principle of market economy: reducing GHG emissions can be done in different ways, and according to local specific circumstances there are cheaper and more expensive ways. Somebody for whom cutting their own emissions is expensive or not feasible might be tempted to pay someone else to reduce theirs instead. Accessing cheaper reductions allows you to set more aggressive targets overall, and benefits the countries where reductions are being funded. Economists say that demand and supply will regulate the price: the more firms, countries and individuals seek to reduce their emissions, but opt for helping others to reduce their emissions by paying for it rather than taking direct measures, the higher the price for a reduction will become, until the point where reducing the own emissions will become cheaper than buying emission certificates for offsets.

Although voluntary action is already contributing to slow down the increase of GHGs in the atmosphere, a widely accepted binding limit of maximum allowed emissions, with appropriate consequences in case of non-compliance, would make the concept far more effective. This is already the case – in theory – for members of the Kyoto Protocol who committed to national emission targets by 2012. These targets can be reached by a combination of reducing national emissions and the use of the "Flexibility Mechanisms" which also include offsetting GHG emissions under certain conditions offsetting mechanisms approved by the Kyoto Protocol. But many countries are not on track reaching national emission targets, partly due to the fact that they have internally not enforced binding limits to their subjects.

Registries

Carbon offset registries keep track of offsets and are vital in minimizing the risk of double-counting (that is, to have multiple stakeholders take credit for the same offset.) Registries also clarify ownership of offsets. A serial number is assigned to each verified offset. When an offset is sold, the serial number and "credit" for the reduction is transferred from the account of the seller to an account for the buyer. If the buyer "uses" the credit by claiming it as an offset against their own emissions, the registry retires the serial number so that the credit cannot be resold.

A cheap way to wash off your sins?

Offsetting can claim several pluses. It raises people's awareness of the issue, promotes sustainable technologies (e.g. through funding for renewable energy projects), and can offer development benefits to local communities. Above all, it reduces GHG emissions, if done correctly. But there are also inescapable drawbacks, and offsetting has some determined opponents. It is a cheap and easy way to salve your conscience without actually doing anything at all, they argue. If you can simply pay a little for the promise of future climate innocence, it will do nothing to persuade you to cut your emissions radically in the here and now. Even if the overall amount of emissions is reduced by the offsets, structures that are linked to the emissions generated in the first place remain without improvement (for example inefficient public transport systems). Inequality between those who can afford to emit and those who cannot is yet another criticism that offset supporters have to face. Carbon Trade Watch (www.carbontradewatch.org) describes offsets as "modern day indulgences, sold to an increasingly carbon-conscious public to absolve their climate sins."

And what about future value accounting? This arises when you are sold an offset today which will actually take some time to act before the emissions are reduced. This can lead to a buyer thinking wrongly that they have already offset their emissions. And the longer the project takes to make the reduction, the more chance there is of something going wrong, with the offset perhaps never actually being achieved.

To counter these arguments, supporters of offsets argument that compared to indulgences, offsets are more than just useless promises on paper; they actually do help in saving the climate. And given that there are binding emissions targets in place, rising prices for offsets resulting from both, increasing demand as well as growing economic development, cutting our own emissions will eventually be more attractive. Maybe not immediately but definitely sooner if we all participate.

The most desirable way of reducing emissions will in most cases be just that – to reduce emissions. This should always be the first step: Reduce as much as you can. But if you concede that the best is sometimes not a choice at all, for financial or other good reasons, then: Offset the remainder.

What are the offsetting options?

The concept of paying for emissions cuts instead of making a reduction yourself is originally linked to emissions trading. Project-based emissions reductions generated under the official mechanism of the Kyoto protocol are regulated by a strict formal and legal framework and primarily intended to help countries to meet their emission targets. However, these emission reductions can be bought and used by anyone to reduce their climate footprint. Emission reductions which comply with those criteria constitute the compliance market. Although the compliance market makes up the biggest chunk of emission reduction via offsets today, there is also the so-called voluntary market where you can buy offsets that are not eligible under the Kyoto protocol but not necessarily less efficient.

Internal activities which take place within an entity some claim as offsets. For example company x or city y accounts a certain amount of trees they have planted for emissions reduction on their climate balance. As with many activities which have no firewall through external control, it is difficult to check if these activities are as effective as assumed.

Therefore, we will focus on official offsets – allowed under the Kyoto Protocol – and voluntary offsets. Both types can be easily purchased be individuals, organizations and countries.

Compliance market
Legally binding systems seek to persuade actors to reduce their greenhouse gas emissions based on a simple idea: making people pay for polluting will increase the cost of emissions and that will in turn reduce the amount of emissions generated. On this note the Kyoto Protocol provides mechanisms that allow parties to reduce emissions outside their

own country but to account for their national emission reduction targets. Offsets offered and purchased under this framework are part of the "compliance market". For all offsets created under the Kyoto mechanisms it is independently verified that the reductions have actually taken place and registered in the Clean Development Mechanism (CDM) registry which has the advantage of transaction credibility, protection against fraud and errors, and simplified facilitation of transactions based on established standards and procedures.

In 1997 the Kyoto Protocol established legally-binding targets for greenhouse gas reductions by the so-called Annex I countries (predominantly developed countries and countries with economies in transition). The Protocol established what are called Flexible Mechanisms to allow these countries to meet their targets by trading carbon credits or emission reduction units – essentially this means buying the right to emit from those with emission rights to spare. Emission reductions can be achieved through the 'Clean Development Mechanism' (CDM) and 'Joint Implementation' (JI). The compliance market is the product of these Flexible Mechanisms. International 'Emissions Trading' is an option under which most Annex I countries can supplement domestic reductions by trading spare GHG emission quotas with each other.

Clean Development Mechanism (CDM)

The CDM is expected to have delivered close to three thousand million tonnes of CO_2e in offsets by 2012 which makes it the framework generating the largest number of emission reductions in the world. It allows Annex I countries to invest in projects that reduce emissions in developing countries as an alternative to more expensive emission reductions in their own countries to meet their own reduction targets. The projects generate emissions credits called Certified Emissions Reductions (CERs), which can then be traded. Anyone, not only governments, can buy the CDM certificates and use them to meet their obligations under the Kyoto Protocol. For the countries where the projects take place, the investment results in various benefits such as technology transfer and economic stimulus. To date there are almost 1 000 projects registered under the CDM mechanism. In order to qualify for the CDM, one must demonstrate that the activities result in additional emissions reductions.

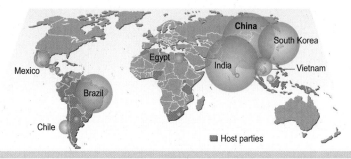

Certified Emission Reduction units issued by host parties

Million CERs

40
20
5
1

Certified Emission Reductions

One certified emission reduction unit is equivalent to a one-tonne reduction in greenhouse gas emissions (measured in CO_2 equivalent).

Circles have only been drawn for countries that have issued more than 50,000 CERs.

China
South Korea
Egypt
India
Vietnam
Mexico
Brazil
Chile

■ Host parties

Source: United Nations Framework Convention on Climate Change, April 2008.

In order to qualify for the CDM, activities have to ensure that the emission reductions are strictly **_additional_** and that they contribute to sustainable

"Additionality" means the projects must achieve cuts in emissions that would not have happened otherwise. If a scheme to cut air pollution also brings about a reduction in GHG emissions, for example, then the cut would have occurred anyway, as a by-product, and there is no additionality. To try to avoid giving credits to projects like this ("free riders"), there are some rules which try to ensure the project does in fact reduce emissions more than would have happened in any case.

development in the host country. Emission reductions created through CDM projects are considered to be of very high quality due to the strict requirements to be approved under the CDM and which is ensured by quality control and independent third party evaluation. However, since the cost to certify and meet all the criteria are considerable, the price for an offset unit created under the CDM is often more expensive than outside the compliance market.

All project types are in general eligible to be certified as CDM (under the precondition that they are located in Non-Annex I countries) and lead to re-

Registered projects implemented under Kyoto's "Clean Development Mechanism"

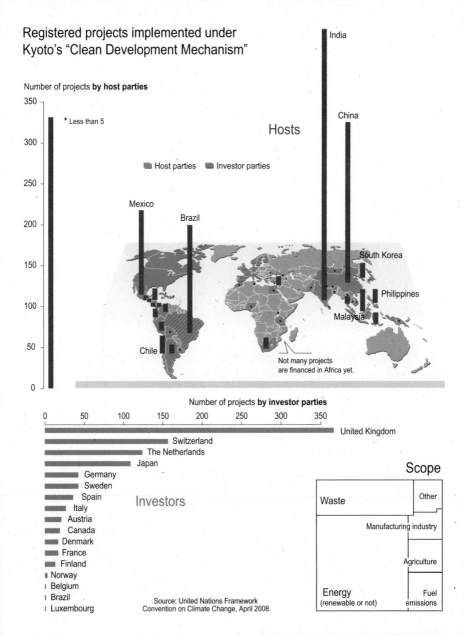

Number of projects **by host parties**

* Less than 5

Hosts

■ Host parties ■ Investor parties

India

China

Mexico

Brazil

South Korea

Philippines

Malaysia

Chile

Not many projects
are financed in Africa yet.

350
300
250
200
150
100
50
0

Number of projects **by investor parties**

0   50   100   150   200   250   300   350

United Kingdom
Switzerland
The Netherlands
Japan
Germany
Sweden
Spain
Italy
Austria
Canada
Denmark
France
Finland
Norway
Belgium
Brazil
Luxembourg

Investors

Scope

Waste		Other
	Manufacturing industry	
		Agriculture
Energy (renewable or not)		Fuel emissions

Source: United Nations Framework
Convention on Climate Change, April 2008.

Cultivating one hectare of wheat

3 020

duction of GHGs under the Kyoto Protocol. Excluded are projects related to nuclear energy, new HCFC-22 facilities and avoided deforestation. Typical activities under the CDM comprise:

- Renewable energy projects, such as: wind, solar, geothermal, (clean) biomass and hydro energy.
- Energy efficiency improvement projects.
- Transportation improvement projects.
- Projects concerning recovery and utilisation of methane, for example from waste landfills or coal mines.
- Projects concerning fossil fuel switching to less carbon-intensive sources.
- Afforestation and reforestation

Joint Implementation (JI)

JI is very similar to CDM; one country invests in emissions reduction projects that take place in another country. As under the CDM, projects must demonstrate additionality and go through a similar verification and certification process. The main difference is that JI operates in other Annex I countries instead of developing countries. Unlike host countries of CDM projects, countries that host JI projects have committed themselves under the Kyoto Protocol to legally binding reduction targets. These projects generate tradable credits which are called Emission Reduction Units (ERUs) also equivalent to one tonne of carbon. Most JI projects are expected to take place in so-called "economies in transition," currently Russia and Ukraine are slated to host the greatest number of JI projects. As with emission certificates from CDM projects, JI certificates can be purchased by anyone interested in offsetting.

The Emissions Trading Scheme

For countries that are signatories to the Kyoto Protocol and with legally binding emission targets, a tool to help them is the **Emissions Trading Scheme**. This is a so-called cap-and-trade scheme, which means countries are allowed a certain amount of emissions which should decrease over time to achieve overall emission reduction. In the Kyoto scheme each allowance is called an Assigned Amount Unit (AAU), equivalent to one tonne of carbon dioxide. These allowances are tradable among countries. At the end of a set period each country must hold the same amount of AAUs as it has emitted tonnes of greenhouse gases. In case the country emitted more, they can add to the AAUs offsets that have been created under the Kyoto Protocol mechanisms in order to balance the additional emissions. This is where the CERs, ERUs and Removal Units from Carbon sinks (RMUs), etc. play their role.

Accounting units

Each one equals one tonne of CO_2 equivalent

A A U	Assigned Amount Unit	Emission allowance allocated to a country under the Kyoto Protocol
C E R	Certified Emission Reduction	Emission reduction expected from a Clean Development Mechanism (CDM) project
R M U	Removal Unit	Emission reduction from land use, land-use change and forestry activities resulting from a CDM or a Joint Implementation (JI) project
E R U	Emission Reduction Unit	Emission reduction from a JI project
V E R	Voluntary Emission Reduction	Emission reduction from a voluntary project not bound to any legal framework or standard

(VER also means "Verified Emission Reduction", an acceptable unit for Chicago Climate Exchange contracts, but not Kyoto)

Emissions Trading offers the choice whether to take possibly unpopular steps at home, like restricting road traffic, or to pay another country to cut its emissions instead. A deal like that may mean the emissions can be reduced more cheaply.

There are **regional emissions trading schemes** with similar objectives but

In Australia the New South Wales government has set up the NSW Greenhouse Gas Abatement Scheme to reduce emissions from the electricity sector by requiring generators and large users to buy NSW Greenhouse Abatement Certificates (NGACs) to offset part of their GHG emissions. This has led to the free distribution of energy-efficient compact fluorescent light bulbs and other energy efficiency measures, with the cost met by the credits generated. The scheme has made possible the creation and trading of verifiable greenhouse abatement certificates.

In 2003 New York State obtained commitments from nine Northeast US states to form a cap-and-trade CO_2 emissions programme for power generators, called the Regional Greenhouse Gas Initiative, or RGGI. That year also saw corporations begin voluntarily trading GHG emission allowances on the Chicago Climate Exchange. In 2007, the California Legislature passed a bill aimed at curbing carbon emissions. California is one of five states and one Canadian province that have joined to create the Western Climate Initiative, aiming to set up a regional GHG control and trading environment.

not identical to the Emissions Trading under the Kyoto protocol. The largest is the EU Emissions Trading Scheme **(EU ETS)**. It is different from

The EU ETS issues trading units called EU Allowances (EUAs) which are comparable to the AAU under the Kyoto Protocol. Today, there is common understanding that caps during the first phase of the EU ETS from 2005 to 2007 have been set too large, with the consequence that prices for CO_2 certificates are too low to provide any incentive to reduce emissions. In January 2008, the European Commission proposed a number of changes to the scheme, including centralized allocation (no more national allocation plans), a turn to auctioning a greater share of emission permits rather than allocating freely. They also included the greenhouse gases nitrous oxide and perfluorocarbons. Moreover, the proposed caps foresee an overall reduction of greenhouse gases for the sector of 21 per cent in 2020 compared to 2005 emissions. Today the price within the ETS lies around 25 Euros per tonne CO_2 compared to below 10 Euro cents in late 2007.

the Flexibility Mechanism in a way that here companies (not countries) in certain emission-intensive sectors such as power generation and cement are assigned a certain amount of emissions by the countries. The latter are required to reduce them over time since the number of allowances decreases from one period to the next, that is basically what cap-and-trade means. However the EU linked the EU ETS to the Flexible Mechanisms of the Kyoto Protocol by allowing a certain number of emissions reductions created under CDM or JI projects to be used and traded at the EU ETS.

The voluntary market

Beyond the CDM and JI, there is the growing unofficial offset industry, a range of both charitable and profit-making groups which broker offsets. Since emission reduction projects under the Kyoto protocol carry a huge responsibility, the criteria they have to comply with in order to be eligible are very strict and for some type of projects not at all achievable. This is one reason why projects and related emission reductions are also created outside the compliance market which can be purchased on the "voluntary market". But they cannot be used for Emissions Trading under the Kyoto Protocol. However, there is a legally-binding voluntary market where parties can set self-imposed, legally binding greenhouse gas emissions reductions targets the Chicago Climate Exchange *(CCX)*.

The CCX was launched in 2003 and is a voluntary, legally binding integrated trading system to reduce emissions of the six major greenhouse gases with offset projects worldwide. CCX employs independent verification, and has been trading greenhouse gas emission allowances since 2003. The companies joining the exchange commit to reducing their aggregate emissions by 6 per cent by 2010. To date the exchange has more than 350 members.

Registries, which are usually set up for a specific system, have been developed for the voluntary market by governments, non-profits, and the private sector, but often not yet applied. Some of the registries are tied to certain standards whereas others function independently. Most voluntary standard registries are still in the planning stage and not yet operational.

The voluntary market is still new but appears to be growing fast. The Climate Group estimates that it doubled to trade in about 20 Megatonnes (Mt) of CO_2 equivalent in 2006, a figure it expects to grow to around 400 Mt CO_2 equivalent by 2010. In the voluntary market there are no overarching or compulsory standards or methodologies for creating credits. There are, however, a number of voluntary standards emerging in an attempt to bring greater robustness and harmonization to the voluntary offset marketplace.

Carbon offset standards

There have been many problems with the carbon offset market, and in particular with the voluntary market, in the past.

One problem is that the offset industry lacking transparency. Some excellent offset projects do address climate change, help wildlife and ecosystems and produce social benefits, but others have little or nothing to show for all their claims. Beyond that, the price of an offset for a specified amount of carbon can vary wildly between different companies. The offset industry offers a variety of calculations and prices for what sometimes appears to be the same activity.

Where carbon registries are missing, double counting can arise when several people try to take the credit for the GHG emissions reduced by one project. This can occur unintentionally through bad management of a project with a bad audit trail, or deliberately when somebody tries selling a credit more than once – a fraudulent act.

Projects sometimes simply fail, in both the compliance market as well as in the voluntary market. In one famous case 40 per cent of the trees in an offset plantation died because not enough water was made available to support the project. The same sort of thing can happen when a project causes unintended damage. For example, if a forestry scheme uses a significant amount of a local water supply, this can damage local agriculture and people's ability to grow crops outside the project.

Another trap to beware of is that your project should not be to the detriment of the people "profiting from it". One example reported involved a project which was accused of working only because people were obliged to use low technology to avoid emitting CO_2 – hand-powered pumps relying for energy on human muscles, which critics said perpetuated underdevelopment. The project's supporters, though, said the people using the pumps had deliberately chosen them.

When looking at the wide range of projects, providers and locations of offsetting projects, you would probably appreciate some guidance in this offset-jungle. In particular with voluntary offsets, where there is no unified

Flight Paris-New York and return (average emission per passenger)

3 670

framework on methodologies or verification, a number of standards have been created over the past year. Not only voluntary offsets but also CDMs, which are already a quality label in themselves, have been subject to further quality specification, for example under the widely recognized Gold Standard. Over a dozen voluntary offset standards have been developed in the last few years. Yet no single standard has so far managed to establish itself as *the* industry standard. Certain standards are limited to particular project types (e.g.forestry), while others exclude some project types in order to focus on the social benefits of carbon projects.

Among the biggest are the Gold Standard for CDM and JI, the Gold Standard for Voluntary Emission Reductions and the Voluntary Carbon Standard (VCS).

The Gold Standard

In 2003 the Gold Standard for CDM and JI (GS CDM) projects was developed under the leadership of the WWF and was followed by the Gold Standard for Voluntary Emission Reductions (GS VER) in 2006. The Gold Standard is generally accepted as the standard with the most stringent quality criteria.

The Gold Standard for CDM is built on the foundations of CDM standards and methodologies, but requires explicit social and environmental benefits of its carbon offset projects which need to prove their sustainable development achievements. Projects are restricted to renewable energy and end-use energy efficiency, thus promoting a fundamental shift in energy use while promoting local economies. It excludes large hydropower projects above 15 MW capacity.

In 2006 the Gold Standard for voluntary offsets was established in order to provide the possibility to have certified projects outside the compliance market. Although the Gold Standard was not strictly for CDM projects, the use of CDM standards as a foundation (which are costly to meet) means that few projects outside of the compliance market are attracted to it. The Gold Standard VER still builds on the criteria applied for Gold Standard CDM projects but the main differences are:

- Simplified guidelines for "micro"-projects delivering less than 5 000 t of emission reductions annually, significantly lowering transaction costs
- Broader eligibility of host countries
- Lower requirements on the use of official development assistance (ODA)
- Broader scope of eligible baseline methodologies
- No need for formal host country approval

Gold Standard VER projects cannot be implemented in countries with an emissions cap, except if the emission reductions are backed by AAUs being permanently retired. In all ten projects have been registered under the Gold Standard. About 35 projects are official Gold Standard Applicants, representing about 4 million CERs and 500 000 VERs. Another 65+ projects are in the pipeline.

CERs are registered in the CDM registry and will be tracked in the Gold Standard registry as well. VERs will be registered in the Gold Standard registry which will be launched in early 2008.

The Gold Standard Foundation is a non-profit organization under Swiss Law, funded by public and private donors.

Voluntary Carbon Standard

The Voluntary Carbon Standard (VCS) is to provide a credible but simple set of criteria to confirm the integrity projects on voluntary carbon market.

A second version of the standard was launched in November 2007 (VCS 2007). It is broadly supported by the carbon offset industry. It will likely become one of the more important standards in the voluntary offset market and might very well establish itself as the main standard for voluntary offsets.

The VCS is a global standard applicable to all project types in all jurisdictions except for any **HFC projects**, nuclear power projects and hydro power

HFC-23 is generated as an unwanted by-product during the manufacture of HCFC-22, a widely used refrigerant. HFC-23 is a very powerful greenhouse gas about 11 700 times more powerful than carbon dioxide but it is quite easy to destroy. A small investment in process changes in aging factories can easily destroy the gas. The global carbon industry has been accused of making these small investments obscenely profitable, with the consequence that due to the low prices for those offsets, investments are missing for sustainable projects such as renewable energy and energy efficiency, as they are far less profitable. Supposedly, investment in the destruction of HFC-23 has even encouraged the production of the chemical in order to benefit from the international contributions. However the system in general is not to blame. Cheaper ways to reduce the climate impact will be accessed first. That is how the market mechanism works, once the easy options are "used up", the market will proceed to slightly more costly options.

Today HFC-23 projects are excluded from various standards; they are however still eligible for the CDM process even though it is currently negotiated whether to rule out such projects from the international climate regime.

projects exceeding 80 MW. Hydro power projects exceeding 20 MW are only approved when they comply with the criteria set by the World Commission on Dams.

The aim of the VCS is to provide a degree of standardization to the voluntary carbon market and to achieve "real, measurable, permanent, additional, independently verified, and not double-counted" emission reductions. The VCS has created a tradable unit called the Voluntary Carbon Unit (VCU). To manage the emissions reductions under the VCS, the organization has created a registry managed by the Bank of New York which is used to register, transfer and retire VCUs from the market.

As VCS 2007 was only launched at the end of 2007, it is difficult to determine how many projects have been certified since the system is still under development. The VCS Association expects that between 50–150 projects creating between 10–20 million tonnes of CO_2 equivalent will have been approved under the VCS Programme by the end of 2008.

The VCS was developed by the International Emissions Trading Association (IETA), The Climate Group (TCG), the World Business Council for Sustainable Development (WBCSD) and the World Economic Forum (WEF).

Further reading:
A report was published in March 2008 by the WWF which explains main criteria and compares carbon offset standards: http://assets.panda.org/downloads/vcm_report_final.pdf.

How to choose?

Customers in the non-legally binding voluntary market are able to purchase both credits which originate from the compliance market and credits which originate from the voluntary market. This means if you are not required by law to buy offsets that are recognized by the Kyoto Protocol (from CDM of JI projects) other legally binding systems such as the Chicago Climate Exchange you have the free choice what to go for. Criteria you may want to consider are reliability, additional benefits such as sustainability and environmental benefits, price and compatibility of the project with your own interests. For example a shipping company might find it more attractive to invest in a marine project than in a tree planting project, or maybe you would prefer to invest in a portfolio rather than in a single project. Together with the standards described above and others, offset providers and brokers should be able to give the relevant information you need.

A widely cited report on carbon offset providers prepared by the Tufts Climate Initiative is available at www.tufts.edu/tie/tci/pdf/TCI_Carbon_Offsets_Paper_April-2-07.pdf. Other websites that compare offset companies are for example The Carbon Catalogue, www.carboncatalog.org/providers; or EcoBusinessLinks, www.ecobusinesslinks.com/carbon_offset_wind_credits_carbon_reduction.htm.

The table on pages 176–177 summarizes the findings from the Tufts Climate Initiative report and also includes recommendations on carbon offset providers by the initiative.

Research the options among different offset providers. Read the provider's information carefully and look for quality controls. As competition grows among offset providers, many now offer third party verification, providing assurances that your purchase has the intended impact. You should focus primarily on quality, but you can also consider price. Prices per tonne of CO_2 reduction can range dramatically, from US$5 to US$40. Think about what you are getting for your money, the verification provided, the source of the offsets.

Buy the offset! Most offset providers sell through the Internet, so you'll be able to buy with a credit card and get confirmation of your new clean-living, clean-driving status within minutes. In many cases you will not be able to choose where your money goes to since it is very complicated for offset providers to manage specific requests in large numbers. Starting from around 100 tonnes CO_2 you can find companies that offer to dedicate your contribution to a particular project. Depending on your lifestyle and how much you manage to reduce in the first place, this may account for several years to decades you could compensate with this.

Apart from approaching an offset provider by yourself, some companies offer you to buy the offset together with their product. The question is whether it would not make more sense if they did automatically include the offsetting cost in their products. But that of course needs to be answered by the customers who are willing to pay a higher price for a **climate neutral product**.

Half a kilo of salmon, two kilos of potatoes – and a tonne of greenhouse gas reductions? Shoppers at one Norwegian mall can now buy cuts in their climate footprint as they pick up their weekly groceries. The Stroemmen Storsenter shopping centre outside Oslo has begun selling certificates at 165 Norwegian crowns (US$30.58) per tonne to people who feel bad about contributing to climate change. The mall's managers said the certificates were bought by individuals and by small firms wanting them for their employees. Each Norwegian accounts for about 11 tonnes of GHGs annually, mainly from burning fossil fuels. "Many people want to buy reductions, but until we started this in the shopping mall they haven't known where to get them..." said Ole Herredsvela, the centre's technical manager. "We are doing this also to create awareness among people towards the problem (of climate change)," he said. Norway's third-biggest shopping centre is not making money from the sales, but is selling them at cost plus a 10 per cent administration fee which goes to its partner, Norwegian carbon management services firm CO_2 focus.

Offset providers

● Non-profit ○ Profit

	Accuracy of air travel emissions calculator	Standards and verification	Project location
● atmosfair	Excellent	CDM, Gold Standard	International
○ Climate friendly	Excellent	Green Power, Gold Standard	International and domestic
● Myclimate (Swiss site)	Very good	Gold Standard	International and domestic
● Myclimate (US site)	Acceptable (some underestimates)	Gold Standard	International
○ NativeEnergy	Very good	Green-e, Climate Neutral Network	Domestic
● CarbonCounter	Very good	Climate Trust	International and domestic
○ Carbonfund	Underestimates	CCX, Green-e, ERT	International and domestic
○ The CarbonNeutral Company	Underestimates	Voluntary Carbon Standard version 1	International and domestic
○ Climate Care	Underestimates	NA	International
○ Offsetters	Underestimates	NA	International
○ TerraPass	Underestimates	Green-e, CCX, CRS	Domestic
○ Better World Club	No calculator	N/A	Domestic
○ Cleanairpass	No calculator	CCX	International and domestic
○ Solar Electric Light Fund	No calculator	N/A	International

Type of projects	Price per tonne of CO_2 offset	% of money to projects	Recommended
Renewables, energy efficiency	US$17.30	80%	Yes
Renewables	US$14.50	66%	Yes
Renewables, energy efficiency	US$112 (Swiss projects) $38	80%	Yes
Renewables, energy efficiency	US$18.00	80%	Yes
Renewables	US$12.00	N/A	Yes
Renewables, energy efficiency	US$10.00	90%	with reservations
Renewables, energy efficiency	US$5.50	93%	with reservations
Renewables, energy efficiency, sequestration, methane capture	US$18.40 (including VAT) 17.5% (including VAT)	60%	with reservations
Renewables, energy efficiency, sequestration	US$12.57	60%	with reservations
Energy efficiency, sequestration	US$13.03	65%	with reservations
Renewables, energy efficiency	US$10.00	N/A	with reservations
Energy efficiency	US$11.00	N/A	No
Renewables, energy efficiency, Sequestration	US$7.982	25%	No
Renewables	US$10.00	N/A	No

Source: *Evaluations and Recommendations of Voluntary Offset Companies*, Tufts Climate Initiative, 2006

In the future, new concepts such as **Personal Carbon Trading**, carbon label-

> *Personal Carbon Trading refers to the act of equally allocating emissions credits to individuals on a per capita basis, within national carbon budgets (for an example of how this would work, see the United Kingdom Climate Change Bill). Individuals would probably hold their emissions credits in electronic accounts and surrender them when they made carbon-related purchases, such as electricity, heating fuel and petrol. People wanting more energy would be able to take part in emissions trading to secure more credits, just as companies do now within the EU ETS. There are no working schemes at the moment. Current proposals include Tradable Energy Quotas – which would bring other sectors of society (e.g. industry) within the scope of the scheme – and Personal Carbon Allowances. These proposals could be applied on a national or multinational basis. Proponents of personal carbon trading claim it could increase "carbon literacy", helping people to make a fair contribution to reducing CO_2 emissions (and ultimately those of other GHGs). It could allow the burden of reducing emissions to be shared evenly throughout the economy, rather than focusing all the attention on business and governments, and could encourage more localized economies.*

ling or integrated offsets will certainly receive further attention.

Easy offset

When you buy a ticked on the EasyJet airline website and before the flight is booked, you are asked if you would like to offset the emissions from the flight you are just about to purchase. The offsets offered by the company are CERs created from CDM projects. The non-profit scheme works fairly easy. The airline calculates the carbon emitted from the passenger flight and buys an equivalent share from a range of CERs. By avoiding any middle-man and buying directly from the pool of offsets available the company can keep the cost low and forward this advantage to its customers.

The projects supported by this scheme range from biomass to wind farms. One project for example supported by EasyJet customers is the construction of the Perlabi hydropower plant that uses water from Chirizacha River in the Andes in Ecuador, South America. The emission reduction in the first decade is expected to be about 74 000 tonnes. The project generates clean electricity, reducing reliance on fossil fuel power generation as well as creating benefits and job opportunities to the local community.

Offset while you work

A company called Vebnet, which supplies technology and support services for employee benefits, has announced a service enabling 250 000 UK employees to help combat climate change directly through their monthly pay. In partnership with PURE – the Clean Planet Trust, individuals can calculate their emissions online and compensate the environment for their own CO_2 pollution by "giving as they earn" through the flexible benefits programme provided by their employer. By combining PURE's and Vebnet's online technology, employees from 170 UK companies can take responsibility for their household and travel emissions, offsetting all or part in monthly payments from their pay.

SMALLER ORGANIZATIONS

For organizations in general, to offset their emissions they have to decide whether they are worried about direct emissions generated during operations; product life-cycle emissions, linked to a product from cradle to grave; or emissions arising from a specific activity, such as business travel or commuting. These questions should be answered by the GHG inventory that is in the beginning of the process. Among others, one GHG calculator especially developed for businesses is at www.safeclimate.net/calculator. For non-individuals, online calculators from offset providers on their websites are in most cases not specific enough. However, many offset providers offer their services in helping to calculate the emissions to their customers.

Depending on the amount of offsets you need to purchase, you might want to choose the type of project you would like to invest in. As mentioned above, commonly there is a certain minimum amount required, but it might be worth looking into that option in the interest of your organization or for advertizing your efforts.

The GHG emissions of the FIFA World Cup in 2006 in Germany were entirely compensated with carbon offsets that were financed by the sponsors of the event and the FIFA. Until then it was the biggest single offsetting project and it was executed by MyClimate in Switzerland. It was requested that the emissions reduction projects should regard environmental and sustainability concerns and take place in South Africa, the host country of the FIFA World Cup in 2010. For compensating the GHG emissions two Gold Standard CDM projects were selected to offset emissions of the world's largest sport event: a fuel-switching project in the Limpopo Province, and a biogas project in the Johannesburg area.

The main concerns are whether buying credits will actually produce results, and whether customers and other stakeholders will be impressed, therefore purchasing high quality offsets will most likely yield highest benefits although their prices may be higher. But the benefits of showing leadership on climate change may appear to balance out the worries. Even small organizations wield considerable economic clout, which means they can influence the offset projects they choose by bringing far more money to bear than an individual offsetter.

⊚ LARGER ORGANIZATIONS

For companies that are required by law to compensate extra emissions it makes most sense to purchase offsets from the compliance market. This is for example the case for the more than 10 000 plants for power generation, iron and steel, glass, cement, pottery and bricks across Europe that fall under the EU Emissions Trading Scheme (EU-ETS). For others the act of offsetting emissions from their entire operations, or part of them, is voluntary but often has a lot of benefits. However, companies do need to remember the insistence of the critics that emissions must be reduced, not just offset, otherwise offsetting becomes a form of "greenwash." Offsets are just one part of a corporate climate strategy, chosen after all possible reductions have taken place.

Since larger organizations naturally tend to have more emissions, they might consider other options for offsetting them, mainly because they may be able to get better offers by being a large investor. As shown in the EasyJet example earlier in the text, when you are able to buy considerable amounts, offsets can also be purchased directly from project developers or marketplaces where they trade their emission reductions. This will save you from paying the overheads of all the brokers that handle the offsets between the project and the retailer.

Emissions from one tonne of **paper waste** going to disposal (no recycling, no recovery)

1 470

Emissions from one tonne of **food waste** going to disposal (no recovery)

1 060

Another option would be that large organizations implement their own emissions reduction project, most likely in a field they are already active in, for example a power company that develops a renewable energy project in a developing country which would then be certified according to CDM criteria or verified by another credible standard. That way the company can benefit from the technological experience and take credits for the project benefits plus save cost by keeping as much as possible of the investment in house.

One corporation that thinks offsets are worthwhile is the HSBC Group, which says it is the world's first carbon-neutral major bank. Its carbon management plan includes managing and reducing its direct emissions, buying "green electricity", and offsetting its other emissions. It bought 170 000 tonnes of carbon offset credits from a New Zealand wind farm, an Australian organic waste composting scheme, an agricultural methane capture project in Germany, and an Indian biomass co-generation plant.

More and more firms now accept the concept as a way of showing how green they are. Their motives may include ethical conviction, compliance with voluntary and mandatory targets, product branding and stakeholder pressure. They may also fear the threat of legislation and want to persuade government that regulations are not needed. Whatever their reasons, they are economically still more powerful than small organizations- powerful enough to set up their own projects, and to direct the transfer of technology and capacity building.

CITIES

For Cities basically the same principles apply as for organizations. First and foremost you would want to ensure the quality of your offsets, that they are truly additional, not double-counted and promote sustainable development in the area where they are implemented.

Depending on the amount of offsets you are planning to purchase in order to eliminate the remainder of your emissions, you might consider going through an offset provider which will be quite convenient. Choosing a particular project that is easily understandable and with obvious benefits to the climate, local people and the environment will help to include your citizens and communicate what offsets are and how they work.

Larger cities might be interested in the option of purchasing directly from project developers or even create their own projects as described for large organizations.

COUNTRIES

Through the Kyoto Protocol mechanisms countries are bound to the compliance market if they want offsets to be accounted on their emissions balance under the legal framework.

Countries play an important role in bringing forward the whole system of carbon offsetting. In order to improve the whole system for mandatory and voluntary offsets a country can do even more than a city to raise standards in the industry, both by what it decides to do nationally and by working for effective international regulation. Obvious examples are the countries which were the first to join UNEP's Climate Neutral Network: Costa Rica, Iceland, New Zealand and Norway.

The Holy See (Vatican) is one example of willingness to explore the potential of offsetting, planting a forest in Hungary to compensate for carbon emissions from papal flights. Any city or country can also exert some regulatory power over offset schemes, for example by requiring suppliers to choose only those proven to work.

Evaluate, tell your story, and do it again

So now you have done everything you set out to do, you have taken a giant step towards climate neutrality, and you can just sit back and wait for the rest of the world to follow your lead? Well no, not really. You have taken the first essential step, and you have every right to be pleased that you have. But there's still a long and winding road ahead on the way to a truly climate-neutral life. You have made a start. You now have to assess what you have managed to do so far, to tell people about it, and then to carry on, only this time more effectively.

Evaluate your progress

The obvious reason for evaluating what you have managed to achieve is to make sure you do better next time round. The chances of improving on your performance will be much higher if you know what that performance amounted to. So you owe it to yourself to make an honest appraisal of what you have done. You also owe it to everyone else to let them know of your success (and your mistakes too: they should be given the chance to avoid wasting effort in the ways that you have probably done). It bears repeating: working towards climate neutrality is important not just for what you do yourself, but for the way it shows other people what they can do.

Whether you are an individual, business, city administration or country, evaluation starts with the obvious step of counting by how much you have actually reduced your GHG emissions. But you will want to count the cost of the reductions as well, so you can see how to make the biggest and most effective cuts. At the same time, count how much your GHG cuts have saved you. Luckily, you have already prepared the ground for counting your emissions earlier in the process, and this re-assessment of progress made since the first analysis will take much less time and effort.

And make sure to factor in both direct and indirect benefits. You will have saved energy and reduced your GHG emissions, and you will probably have saved money as well – or, at least, made an investment which will certainly save you money in years to come. But that is only the obvious part. You will have improved your reputation with people you want to impress, and will probably have gained some free advertising as well, a reputation as an individual or company prepared to practice what you preach, which will help to improve your brand image. You may also have avoided legal penalties, and if you are in either local or central government the chances are that you will have earned some electoral popularity. And there is a good prospect that you will have brought about an improvement in health, perhaps your own (from walking instead of driving, for instance), perhaps your community's. Energy not used means pollution not emitted, and lungs and hearts spared damage.

Think as well about what you have learned from this first round of reducing your climate footprint. Probably you will feel you have identified both weak and strong points. If the process has made you more realistic, that will have been worthwhile in itself. You can then start the second round under no illusions. You might want to examine also whether your set-up was ideal, or whether you have to reassign responsibilities among the people involved.

Businesses, cities:

An additional validation of your evaluation is to carry out an audit and get certification for your process in the framework of an environmental management system (GHG protocol certification with ISO 14000 environmental management standards: in ISO 14040:2006 and 14044:2006 for example). This step will improve your credibility and give you extra credits with those you are reporting to: board of trustees, city council, etc.

Tell your story

Perhaps you know someone who has successfully completed a diet, and who cannot stop telling everyone they meet about how much weight they have lost and the privations they had to undergo to do it. That is not really the sort of role model you need, because people like that can be intensely annoying, and are unlikely to persuade many others to emulate them. But at least they do pass the message on, even if they make sure that not many people will absorb it.

Producing one kg of **steel** in Australia 2.3

Producing one kg of **copper** in Australia 5

22 Producing one kg of **aluminium** in Australia

14 Producing one kg of **nickel** in Australia

So learn from them. Let your friends, colleagues, rivals, opponents, casual acquaintances and everyone you can think of know what you have done, how you have managed it, and *why* – there are still people who are not convinced that climate change is real or important. But do it in a way your listeners can hear and understand. Tell them that if you can make the effort, then anybody can. Let them see that what you are doing is rapidly becoming the norm, not the exception.

You probably looked at some of the case studies in earlier chapters, and quite likely you thought they provided useful pointers for you as you embarked on the first phase of reducing your impact on the climate. They inspired you, and now it is your turn to provide inspiration to others.

The effort to become climate-neutral can sometimes arouse incomprehension or even hostility, and if you are accountable to shareholders or employees or voters you may find they expect an explanation from you. It is much better to offer them an explanation before they get round to demanding one. That way you will not sound defensive or apologetic, or as if you are trying to hide something. So telling your story to the people you answer to makes good sense, and may also enlist them to support you and to follow your lead.

INDIVIDUALS

As an individual you are the one category least obliged to market your efforts. That does not mean there is no worthwhile effect from doing so, in particular when your experience might be the first step for others towards climate neutrality. Make sure you tell your family, friends and neighbours for a start. It is also well worthwhile to go back to people whose advice you sought when you started out on the climate-neutral path: tell them what worked for you and what did not, because there is no one-size-fits-all approach. Different strategies work for different people and groups. Reporting back may help your counsellors to refine the advice they give to others who follow you.

What you have begun to do may well have given you a competitive advantage already, and if it has not yet it probably will soon. So you will probably have several alert and eager audiences for the feedback you can provide.

The bigger you are, the more important an organized communication campaign will be to justify the investments that you certainly had to make. Different groups will be interested in different things. Differentiate the information you give out according to the audience it is aimed at. Tell your staff what you are doing, and how it will make the company – their company – more profitable and their families' futures better. Tell your customers how you are (or soon will be) saving money and keeping prices down. Tell your shareholders how you are securing the company's future. Tell your rivals what they are

JOIN THE CLUB –
SUCCESSFUL REPORTING INITIATIVES

Tell everyone who may be interested about the groups that exist specifically to help businesses reduce their emissions. There is the Global Reporting Initiative, which has pioneered the development of the world's most widely-used sustainability reporting framework. This sets out the principles and indicators that organizations can use to measure and report their economic, environmental, and social performance. The cornerstone of the framework is the Sustainability Reporting Guidelines. The third version – known as the G3 Guidelines – was published in 2006, and is available free. Other components of the framework include sector supplements (unique indicators for different industry sectors) and protocols (detailed reporting guidance), and national annexes (unique country-level information). GRI promotes and develops this standardized approach to reporting to stimulate demand for sustainability information, which will benefit both reporting organizations and those who use information from their reports. GRI develops learning materials and accredits training partners, and also provides special guidance for SMEs. More than 1 500 companies worldwide, many of them household names, have announced that they have voluntarily adopted the Guidelines. The GRI is a collaborating centre of the UN Environment Programme.

missing and how everyone gains from reducing their GHG emissions. Tell the community in which you work how your efforts are improving conditions for everyone and offering them – and their children – a healthier future.

Strategic communication

Do not rely simply on spreading the word informally, by word of mouth and chance contacts. By all means write reports and put details on your website, if you think people will read them. Hold a meeting to explain what you have done if you think you can attract a decent audience. Mount a media campaign, because if you can get journalists interested you can inform far more people than by direct contact. Try to get someone from the company invited into schools and to visit groups like local senior citizens' or civic associations. Many of them are always on the lookout for interesting speakers anyway, and nobody is too young – or too old – to start down the climate-neutral road. Hold

Then there is the Carbon Disclosure Project (CDP), which works with shareholders and companies to disclose the companies' greenhouse gas emissions. In 2007 it published the world's largest repository of GHG emissions and energy use data, covering 2 400 of the world's largest corporations, which account together for 26 per cent of global anthropogenic emissions. The CDP represents institutional investors, with a combined US$57 million million under management. Individual governments have been reluctant to develop stringent national emissions limits for fear that big companies will move their factories to nations with laxer regulations. The CDP tries to get round these national interests by focusing on individual companies, not on countries. It unites institutional investors to focus attention on carbon emissions, energy usage and reduction wherever companies and assets are located. Some companies have higher GHG emissions than individual nations. A number have moved to become carbon-neutral, but others can still reduce energy use and emissions by adopting energy efficiency policies and business planning. The CDP has also begun establishing a globally-used standard for emissions and energy reporting. Much of the data it has obtained has never been collected before. An estimated US$27 thousand million will be spent over the next 30 years on energy-related capital developments (new power stations, fuel distillation plants, etc.), so it is vital that the right technologies are adopted.

training sessions for your own staff, and think perhaps of offering incentives (prizes, even) for the best suggestions on ways to change policies and practice to save GHG emissions. What about advertising? You probably do that anyway, so ask your agency to come up with new copy and graphics which will highlight what you are doing. If you feel you have made a real change in seeking to become climate-neutral, and that you have some significant insights to share, then it may be worth commissioning external advisers to take charge of communicating your message as widely and as effectively as possible.

A full-page ad in the largest Swiss Sunday paper drew the attention of readers to the fact that the supermarket chain Migros reduced its CO_2 emissions by 800 000 tonnes. A comprehensive footnote explains that this is counting efforts made since 1990 to improve energy efficiency in stores, optimize logistics, and introduce biogas-fuel lorries among a range of measures taken to reduce energy consumption. The advertisement mentions that the amount saved equals the emissions of 300 000 modern detached houses in one year, offering a comparison comprehensible to most readers.

Not everything Migros does is consistent with its declared responsibility as a sensible energy user. In the same communication campaign, Migros announced more transparency over CO_2 emissions by launching a label for particularly low-emitting products. However, at the same time, their in-house magazine featured a large ad which offered a special discount on seedless grapes from South Africa... This is just one example of a lack of consistency in overall policy and marketing efforts that ought not to hinder the efforts made by this particular company. Nobody's perfect, and everybody starts somewhere and has room for improvement.

Producing one kilogram of beef (average) Producing one kilogram of beef in France

Driving 250 kilometre with an average European car

CITIES

If you are involved in running a city, you have a marvellous opportunity to tell its people what you are doing, why you are doing it, and to inspire them to follow your lead. Use your publicity machine, the reporting tools in your environmental management system, the city's mass media, its NGOs, and international associations of city governments, like the ICLEI network. Use your political contacts to enthuse your colleagues in other cities and towns in your own country. Use the considerable influence you have on your own government.

COUNTRIES

National governments are in a strong position to pass the word on about the opportunities for going climate-neutral, first of all, of course, by the examples they set and the policies they adopt – policies, for instance, on transport, building regulations, the phasing out of perverse subsidies, fiscal encouragement for less GHG-intensive activities and production, and support for international agreements on tackling climate change. They can also shine a spotlight on the need for action by exploiting their ability to convene both national and international conferences and workshops, by using political and historic networks like the OECD, ASEAN, the African Union and the Commonwealth. They can spur national players (cities, NGOs, employers' federations and others) to act, and they can use their public information networks to inform and inspire citizens to emulate national policies in their individual lives.

Producing one tonne of **sugar**

730

Do it all over again

Repeating a fairly difficult process you have just completed does not sound like fun. If you are not in it for the long haul, do not bother: most climate scientists will tell you anyway that even the best efforts at achieving climate neutrality are not guaranteed to work. The rapidity of the onset of change – which, in the words of the IPCC's Fourth Assessment Report, may prove "abrupt and irreversible" – means all bets are off, and we have to try everything we can to avert the worst. But continuing the process for however long is necessary is the best any of us can do if we seriously want to be the change we want to see.

It will be different the second time round. You will have the benefit of greater realism, a clearer understanding of both the difficulties and the potential of what you are doing. You will have a clearer idea, thanks to the lessons you absorbed from your first attempt, of what is likely to work and what is probably not worth bothering about. And by the time you are half-way through this second effort, there is a chance it will be turning into second nature, something it feels quite normal to spend time and effort on doing. In other words, a key element of success is to increasingly automatize and integrate into regular processes many of the functions related to the inventory and assessment. That is the way to equip yourself to make the climate-neutral process a routine, and the routine a way of life that you would not dream of abandoning. This will make future work much easier. That way lies possible success – success that's not guaranteed. But the attempt is better than doing nothing. Nobody begins a diet convinced that it is going to work. They start in hope. That is all we can do in trying to kick the habit of living in a greenhouse gas-dependent society. The job will be hard, but not impossibly so, and the rewards for success make it worth the effort.

Becoming climate-neutral, for many of us as individuals and as consumers, workers, voters, shareholders, or in any other corporate guise, does not need to be the stuff of dreams. It can become a reality in our lives. We shall have to bust a gut to do it, but it is do-able.

KICK THE HABIT
ANNEX

COMPLETE CREDITS

This is a United Nations Environment Programme publication, written and produced by GRID-Arendal at the request of the Environment Management Group

United Nations Environment Management Group
11, Chemin des Anémones, CH-1219 Châtelaine, Switzerland

UNEP/GRID-Arendal
Postboks 183, N-4802 Arendal, Norway

United Nations Environment Programme (UNEP)
United Nations Avenue, P.O. Box 20552, Nairobi, Kenya

The **Environment Management Group (EMG)** is a grouping of all UN agencies and Secretariats of Multilateral Environmental Agreements (MEAs) as well as the Bretton Woods Institutions and the World Trade Organization working together to share information about their respective plans and activities in the fields of environment and human settlements. It was established in 2001 to enhance UN system-wide inter-agency coordination related to specific issues in the field of environment and human settlements. The United Nations Environment Programme (UNEP) hosts the EMG Secretariat located in Geneva, Switzerland. *www.unemg.org.*

UNEP/GRID-Arendal is an official UNEP centre located in Southern Norway. GRID-Arendal's mission is to provide environmental information, communications and capacity building services for information management and assessment. The centre's core focus is to facilitate the free access and exchange of information to support decision making to secure a sustainable future. *www.grida.no.*

The **United Nations Environment Programme (UNEP)** is the world's leading intergovernmental environmental organisation. The mission of UNEP is to provide leadership and encourage partnership in caring for the environment by inspiring, informing, and enabling nations and peoples to improve their quality of life without compromising that of future generations. *www.unep.org.*

Writer:
Alex Kirby

UNEP/GRID-Arendal editorial team:
Jasmina Bogdanovic
Claudia Heberlein
Otto Simonett
Christina Stuhlberger

Copy editing:
Harry Forster, Interrelate Grenoble

Carto-graphics:
Emmanuelle Bournay, UNEP/GRID-Arendal
Cécile Marin, Cartographer
Philippe Rekacewicz, Cartographer

Editorial committee:
Roy Brooke, OCHA
Hossein Fadaei, UN Environment Management Group
Taryn Fransen, World Resources Institute
Audun Garberg, Norwegian Pollution Control Agency
Aniket Ghai, Geneva Environment Network
Christian Kornevall, World Business Council for Sustainable Development
Christian Lambrechts, UNEP DEWA
Judith Moore, The World Bank
Janos Pasztor, UN Environment Management Group
David Simpson, UNEP DCPI
Sudhir Sharma, UNFCCC Secretariat
Maryke van Staden, ICLEI—Local Governments for Sustainability
Niclas Svenningsen, UNEP DTIE
Svein Tveitdal, coordinator editorial committee
Natasha Ward, Inter American Development Bank

Special thanks for collaboration to:
Raul Daussa, OSCE
Remco Fischer, UNEP Finance Initiative
Martina Otto, UNEP DTIE
Philip Reuchlin, OSCE

Content contributors:
Jan Burck, Germanwatch e.V., Germany
James J. Dooley, Joint Global Change Research Institute, United States
Per-Anders Enkvist, McKinsey & Company, Sweden
Mehrdad Farzinpour, Institut du Transport Aérien, France
Daniel Kluge, Verkehrsclub Deutschland e.V., Germany
Stefan Micallef, International Maritime Organization
Ina Rüdenauer, Öko-Institut e.V., Germany
Capt. Eivind S. Vagslid, International Maritime Organization

GLOSSARY

Adaptation
The adoption of policies and practices aimed at preparing for the effects of climate change, accepting that complete avoidance is now impossible because of the inertia of the atmospheric and oceanic systems.

Anthropogenic
Of human origin: used to describe greenhouse gases emitted by human activities.

Carbon dioxide
The main greenhouse gas caused by human activities; it also originates from natural sources, like volcanic activity.

Carbon sequestration and storage
An experimental technology designed to remove carbon dioxide from emissions such as power stations: the gas is then liquified and pumped into rock formations underground or beneath the sea bed. Proponents believe it has great potential for tackling climate change but CCS is not yet available at a commercial stage.

Carbon sink
A natural feature – a forest, for example, or a peat bog – which absorbs CO_2.

CO_2 equivalence
A way of expressing the combined efficiency of all greenhouse gases: carbon dioxide (CO_2), methane (CH_4), nitrous oxide (N_2O), and the rarer trace greenhouse gases such as chlorofluorocarbons. Their potency varies according to their chemical make-up and the length of time they persist in the atmosphere.

Eco-driving
Eco-driving is a way of driving that reduces fuel consumption, greenhouse gas emissions and accident rates.

ISO 14 000
A series of global green standards designed to encourage progress towards sustainable development: developed by the International Organisation for Standardisation. See www.iso.org/iso/home.htm.

Kyoto Protocol
A protocol to the UN Framework Climate Change Convention (see below). The Protocol requires developed countries to reduce their GHG emissions below levels specified for each of them in the Treaty. These targets must be met within a five-year time frame between 2008 and 2012, and add up to a total cut in GHG emissions of at least 5% against the baseline of 1990.

Mitigation
Policies and measures designed to reduce emissions of greenhouse gases so as to mitigate reduce the effects of climate change.

ppm
Stands for 'parts per million' and is the usual measuring unit applied to greenhouse gases because of their relatively small quantities in the atmosphere. 0,0001 per cent is 1 ppm.

Stern Report
The Stern Review on the Economics of Climate Change is a 700-page report written in 2006 by the British economist Sir Nicholas Stern for the UK Government, which discusses the effect of climate change and global warming on the world economy.

UNFCCC
The United Nations Framework Convention on Climate Change (UNFCCC) is the first international climate treaty. It came into force in 1994 and has since been ratified by 189 countries including the United States. More recently, a number of nations have approved an addition to the treaty: the Kyoto Protocol, which has more powerful (and legally binding) measures.

ACRONYMS

ASPO
Association for the Study of Peak Oil and Gas
www.peakoil.net

CAMSAT
Carbon Management Self-Assessment Tool
www.brdt.org/fx.brdt/scheme/camsat.aspx

CCP
Cities for Climate Protection
www.iclei.org/index.php?id=800

CCS
Carbon Sequestration Capture and Storage
http://en.wikipedia.org/wiki/Carbon_capture_and_storage

CDM
Clean Development Mechanism
http://unfccc.int/kyoto_protocol/mechanisms/clean_development_mechanism/
items/2718.php

CN Net
UNEP Climate Neutral Network
www.climateneutral.unep.org/cnn_frontpage.aspx?m=49

C40
C40 Cities Climate Leadership Group
www.c40cities.org

EMAS
Eco-management and audit scheme
http://ec.europa.eu/environment/emas/index_en.htm

GHGs
Greenhouse gases

ICLEI
Local Governments for Sustainability
www.iclei.org